# Screenplay
## by Disney

# Screenplay by Disney

Tips and techniques to bring magic to your moviemaking

Jason Surrell

**Disney EDITIONS**

New York

For information address Disney Editions, 114 Fifth Avenue,
New York, New York 10011-5690.
Visit www.disneyeditions.com

**Disney Editions Editorial Director:** Wendy Lefkon
**Editor:** Jody Revenson
**Design:** Patricia Isaza, Pisaza Design Studio, Ltd.

Academy Award® and Oscar® are registered trademarks of the Academy of Motion Picture Arts and Sciences.

Printed in the United States of America

First Edition

10 9 8 7 6 5 4 3 2 1

Library of Congress Cataloging-in-Publication Data on file.
ISBN: 0-7868-5440-5

**Also by Jason Surrell:**

*The Art of The Haunted Mansion*
*The Haunted Mansion: From the Magic Kingdom to the Movies*
*The Imagineering Way* (contributing essayist)

This book is for Don Hahn, one of the most steadfast keepers of the flame.

THE AUTHOR WOULD LIKE TO THANK THE FOLLOWING PEOPLE for their contributions to this book. At Disney Editions: Christopher Caines, Wendy Lefkon, and Jody Revenson; at the Walt Disney Archives: Dave Smith and Robert Tieman; at Walt Disney Feature Animation: Travis Beckner, Aaron Blaise, Jay Carducci, Ron Clements, Patti Conklin, Dean DeBlois, Roy E. Disney, Joe Grant, Don Hahn, Broose Johnson, Glen Keane, Sanj Marosi, Burny Mattinson, Andrew Millstein, John Musker, Mary-Jane Ruggels, Chris Sanders, Kelly Slagle, David Stainton, Bob Walker, and Chuck Williams.

Special thanks are also due to Kevin Breen, John Canemaker, Michael Farmer, Hunter Heller, Irene Safro, and Jill Safro.

# Table of Contents

# Fade In: A Magical Alchemy••••••••••••••••••••

The legendary screenwriter William Goldman once infamously said of Hollywood, "Nobody knows anything," and people inside and outside the motion picture industry have parroted that infamous maxim ever since, often in the course of explaining away the nonperformance of their own creative endeavors. Goldman's remark is not entirely accurate, nor is it fair. In reality, many people in the industry know a great deal about a good many things. The problem lies in using that knowledge in a way that produces a great film, a work of art that transcends time and taste to take its place among the classics, a film that reaffirms our faith in the medium just when we think we've lost it forever.

The whole is rarely greater than the sum of its parts. When any one of the raw materials used to build a film is of substandard quality or, worse still, actively working against other elements of the construction, the end product will fall in on itself just as surely as the straw and stick houses of the Three Little Pigs did when the Big Bad Wolf blew them down. That is why audiences are often subjected to the mixed message of good performances in middling movies or to briskly edited music videos that run for ninety minutes or more. All too often we see slick entertainments that prize style over substance or films in this age of twenty-first-century visual effects that are feasts for the eyes but mere table scraps for the soul.

The films that do work are the result of a magical alchemy that produces an elixir of life rather than a lethal potion that drains two hours of existence from its victims. They are the gourmet meals that filmmakers create when they somehow manage to use all the right ingredients in just the right way: writing, direction, performance, editing, cinematography, and musical score. Everything is in its proper place and working together toward a common good—a good movie.

A good screen story—and the screenplay through which it is told—may be just one of a film's building blocks, but it is perhaps the most important. If the story does not work in and of itself, none of the work that follows in any of the other disciplines will matter in the slightest, because the foundation itself is bad. If a great film can be considered the result of a magical alchemy, then the screenplay represents in distilled form the larger creative process of which it is such an integral part. A screenplay's components are story, structure, character, and dialogue. In order for their collaborators (director, cinematographer, production designer, and so on) even to have a shot at achieving greatness, screenwriters must bring their work as close to a state of perfection as possible before shooting begins. And just as myriad creative hurdles stand between a film's green light for production and its opening weekend, there are plenty of ill conceptions and bad choices that can throw its script off course along the way. As any aspiring and professional screenwriter knows all too well, every film begins with a blank page or a maddeningly blinking cursor sitting by itself on a lonely computer screen. That is the blessing—and the curse—of storytelling and screenwriting.

Disney's cartoons and animated features have been known to keep even the youngest children remarkably squirm-free in movie theaters, so it's safe to say that the studios have been doing something right for the better part of seventy-five years. They have produced timeless classics that have endured for generations, enchanting untold millions with the magical tales they weave. At other times their creative endeavors have yielded an amusing distraction that enables its audience to forget their cares for a couple of hours—and of most popular entertainment, you can't ask much more than that. And yes, there have been a number of disappointments, creative and financial, films that failed to hit their mark or find an audience. Not even the name *Walt Disney* can ward off all the gremlins that thrive on the sabotage of the art and craft of storytelling. When you take a look at the bigger picture, however, Disney's track record is nothing short of amazing. And there are reasons for that.

A closer look at the animated features can inspire you to tell a better story, too, depending on the kind of story that you want to tell. Disney makes mainstream movies intended for a broad audience—a broad *family* audience, no less—so you're not going to find the structural histrionics of *Pulp Fiction* or the downbeat ending of *Chinatown* in a Disney film. We meet Belle in her quiet village and go on an engrossing—but linear—journey with her; she doesn't tell her story in flashback, already a prisoner in the Beast's castle when we first meet her. At the end of *Aladdin*, Jafar doesn't abscond with Princess Jasmine as the Genie exclaims to the titular hero, "Forget it, Al. It's Agrabah." There's not a lot of gray area or wiggle room between "Once upon a time . . ." and ". . . they lived happily ever after."

When I began my research for this book, I wasn't sure what to expect. I was sure there must be some sort of amazing, well-guarded, and well-worn formula to produce this magical alchemy more often than not. I quickly discovered that there is no formula. Critics and ill-tempered animation fans can snipe all they want about how all of the Disney films seem to rely on a heartfelt "I want" song in the first act or employ some off-the-shelf sidekicks for comic relief. They can accuse the studio of a strict adherence to clichés and conventions, of paint-by-numbers storytelling. It doesn't matter: there is no formula. And I know, because I've looked. There's no magic feather like the one that helped Dumbo to fly. There's no leather-bound book of secrets hidden in a chamber deep beneath Disney's Burbank studio. Believe me, if there were, I would have turned it in to my editor and saved myself a lot of time. And there certainly isn't any kind of "story checklist" tacked to a wall of the executive suite. There are only storytellers and film-makers—creative talent and studio executives alike—who take the Disney tradition very, very seriously.

These storytellers bear closer examination, for there is something of a method to their madness, even if it can't always be easily articulated. The talented men and women (screenwriters and story artists, lead animators and directors, executives and producers) responsible for creating and maintaining the Disney heritage have set an example for all storytellers. Much can be gained by studying the story principles to which they try to adhere, and by examining their overall process, which has emerged over sixty-seven years of producing full-length animated features. Some aspects of that process will seem self-evident; some may come as a surprise to you. You will also begin to discern their indefatigable quest for truth—a dogged determination to remain true to the material, true to themselves and, in the process, true to the audience. Their stories will serve and inspire any story-teller, screenwriters of animated features and live-action films alike, who searches for that magical alchemy.

If you can apply to your own work even a few of the story principles that guide the Disney films, you'll be well on your way to building a solid foundation upon which your future collaborators can erect their own creative structure. And that is no small accomplishment. A great script is the nucleus of a great film, and only the truly great films have a chance of transcending time and taste, as the best of Disney's work has. As a storyteller and a filmmaker, that should be your objective every time you put pen to paper or turn on the computer.

And now, let there be magic. . . .

In the studio's early days, Walt Disney *was* the script. Here he acts out a scene from *Pinocchio* for his story team.

# The Word According to Walt

> *"People are always analyzing our approach to entertainment. Some reporters have called it the 'special secret' of Disney entertainment. Well, we like a little mystery in our films, but there's really no secret about our approach. We're interested in doing things that are fun—in bringing pleasure and especially laughter to people. And we have never lost our faith in family entertainment—stories that make people laugh, stories about warm and human things, stories about historic characters and events, and stories about animals."*

Walt Disney

• • • • • • • • • • • • • • • • • • • • • • • • • • • • • • • • • • • • • • • • •

Like his fellow visionaries who carved Hollywood from the waning frontier, Walt Disney made his first foray into the movie business when the industry was in its early childhood, if not its infancy. It would still be a few years until a certain mouse made his debut, but the young cartoonist from Missouri established early on the creative principles and character-driven approach to story and humor that would guide him throughout his career. Even after his small family business developed into an entertainment empire, Walt never forgot that it was his indomitable faith in the power of story and character that had made it happen.

Most early short cartoons, and many later ones, relied heavily on a series of broad and often violent gags loosely strung together with little discernible attempt at a plot. They were long on slapstick but short on personality; one character could easily be exchanged for another and the audience would scarcely notice the difference. Moviegoers didn't expect much more than that from such petty novelties and amusements, and there really wasn't any compelling reason for them to do so. From his modest start, Walt Disney had something a bit more ambitious and substantial in mind for the short cartoon. Story did not magically or suddenly become part of the Disney way when Walt decided to make the feature-length *Snow White and the Seven Dwarfs* in the mid-1930s. It was the foundation upon which he built his entertainment offerings from the very beginning, and the creation of Mickey Mouse marked the first step of that evolution.

"All we ever intended for him or expected of him," said Walt, "was that he should continue to make people everywhere chuckle with him and at him. We didn't burden him with any social symbolism; we made him no mouthpiece for frustrations or harsh satire. Mickey was simply a little personality assigned to the purposes of laughter."

Mickey may have been "assigned to the purposes of laughter," but Walt made sure that the mouse went about getting those laughs in a wholly new way. He wanted the audience to identify with Mickey as an Everyman and see in him "a little fellow trying to do the best he could." In other words, Walt wanted the audience to recognize *themselves* in the mouse. Only when they did so would they truly see and believe the story Walt was trying to tell them. Mickey (and Minnie, who made her debut right alongside him in 1928's *Steamboat Willie*) became the most well defined animated character of his time, and was quickly followed by a stable of co-stars including his loyal pup, Pluto, in 1932, the Goof, soon to be known and loved as Goofy, in 1930, and the irascible Donald Duck in 1934. These early short cartoons never lacked for humor, but they were composed of much more than a series of broad

> Out of our years of experimenting and experience, we learned one basic thing about bringing pleasure and knowledge to people of all ages and conditions, which goes to the very roots of public communication.
> That is this: the power of relating facts, as well as fables, in story form.
>
> —Walt Disney

gags and violent slapstick. Walt arrived at his laughs honestly, earning them through a new and unique blend of personality and story.

"Walt had found that the real way to get entertainment was through the personalities," says Ollie Johnston, one of Walt's original "Nine Old Men" of animation. "And if you had a gag, why it should be based on what type of personality was involved with it."[1]

Walt's growth as a storyteller continued throughout the 1930s. Audiences truly identified with his characters and believed the stories of which they were a part. The humorous situations in which the characters found themselves and the resulting laughs were a direct result of who the characters *were*. Walt had firmly established each one of his characters as a personality, and from personality he derived believability. And that quality of believability enabled him to tell stories with a beginning, middle, and end. The other animation studios' mindless seven-minute gagfests filled with paper-thin characters and flimsy situations soon became a thing of the past.

Walt quickly pushed the envelopes of character and story with the Silly Symphonies, seventy-five short cartoons produced between 1929 and 1939, which enabled him to make films that didn't feature Mickey Mouse. The Symphonies gave Walt the chance to create new characters whose sole purpose was to be seen and believed at once, without the benefit of their own ongoing series, and to tell one unique, stand-alone story, which very often used a reworking of fairy tales, nursery rhymes, or mythology as their narrative. The Silly Symphonies also helped Walt introduce music as an important storytelling device, something that would only grow in importance in the years to come. These films reached their pinnacle in 1933 with the release of Academy Award winner and audience favorite *Three Little Pigs*, the success of which prompted Walt to exclaim, "At last we have achieved true personality in a whole picture!" But the surest sign of what the future held for Walt Disney and his studio was still four years away.

In a memo distributed in December 1935, Walt said, "I honestly feel that the heart of our organization is the Story Department. We must have good stories—we must have them well worked out—we must have people in there who can not only think up ideas but who can carry them through and sell them to the people who have to do with the completion of the thing. The only way we can develop this Story Department is by starting in and trying to find these people— then we must get them in and try them out—we must try to develop them . . . we must get gagmen who have a little more feeling for situation gags, for personality gags, and who have a little showmanship in their system. They might develop into men who will be capable of carrying a story through to completion."

Throughout the early and mid-1930s, the advances Walt made in the realms of character and story convinced him that audiences would accept a full-length animated feature. By now Walt knew that believability was the key to telling an effective story as well as holding an audience's interest while he told it. Walt's choice for his studio's first feature film was perhaps inevitable.

# Once Upon a Time . . . . . . . . . . . . . . . . . . . . . . . . . . . .

"Come on in the soundstage; I've got something to tell you," Walt told his staff one evening when they returned to the studio from a dinner break. He then proceeded to tell his artists the story of *Snow White and the Seven Dwarfs* from start to finish, acting out all the parts himself.

Legendary Disney animator Ken Anderson, art director on *Snow White* and *Pinocchio*, among other films, remembered that fateful evening: "Walt said, 'I'm going to tell you a story. It's been with me all my life. I've lived it.' Then he started in and told the story of *Snow White* better than we put it on the screen. He spent from eight o'clock to eleven-thirty and he portrayed all the parts. He had to go forward and back and forward and back—the cutting didn't matter—in order to tell it all. But he became the Queen, he became the Huntsman, he became the Dwarfs, he became Snow White. And the guy changed. He sat right in front of our eyes and there was Walt Disney, changing. Now, he had enormous talent as an actor. He could really sell things, and he sold the story to us in such a way that we couldn't believe our ears." [2]

> The success of the Silly Symphonies gave us the courage for Snow White. *And you should have heard the howls of warning! It was prophesied that nobody would sit through a cartoon an hour and a half long. But we had decided that there was only one way we could successfully do it and that was to go for broke— shoot the works. There could be no compromises on money, talent, or time. We did not know whether the public would go for a cartoon feature—but we were darned sure that audiences would not buy a bad cartoon feature.*
>
> —Walt Disney

As a child, Walt had "seen the story and liked it. I thought it was a perfect story. I had the sympathetic dwarfs, you see? I had the heavy; I had the prince and the girl, the romance. I thought it was a good plot and had broad appeal. It wasn't too fantastic. That's what you need: a fairly down-to-earth story that people can associate themselves with."

In *Snow White*, Walt established the two elements that both critics and audiences would point to time and again as hallmarks of the best Disney films: character—or, more specifically, *personality*—and story. The progress he had already made as an artist and storyteller was most evident in 1940, a year that saw the release of his next two animated features, both of which told compelling stories in vastly different ways. One, like *Snow White*, was based on a classic fairy tale; the other used the language of music and little dialogue to interpret a broad range of themes and ideas. It is all the more amazing to consider that a mere twelve years stood between the relative simplicity of *Steamboat Willie* and the artistic and narrative triumphs of *Pinocchio* and *Fantasia*.

*Snow White and the Seven Dwarfs* made motion-picture history and remade the future of The Walt Disney Studios. Short cartoons had gotten them to that point and would remain in production for several more decades, but Walt instinctively knew that feature films would become their new lifeblood. He had proven to critics and audiences alike what he had maintained all along: the believability of his characters, and the illusion of life it helped create, were indeed the keys to sustaining a seventy-minute story and holding the attention of the audience watching it. As film history would bear out, *Snow White* was only the beginning.

The logical question on Walt's mind at that point was, "Where do we go from here?" The answer was, understandably, *anywhere*. Walt and his collaborators had a world of storytelling possibilities at their fingertips. And so do you—as we are about to see.

*"The most important thing brought about in the past quarter century of motion picture history is the recognition that amusement, recreation, mass diversion, is no longer a dispensable luxury. Family fun is as necessary to modern living as a kitchen refrigerator."*

Walt Disney

# Inspiration

> *"Through historical time—and even among our aboriginal forefathers—all the races of man have been dramatizing these eternal quests and conquests of mind and heart; in arenas, around tribal fires, in temples and theaters. The modes of entertainment have changed through the centuries; the content of public shows, very little."*
>
> Walt Disney

We've been telling stories for as long as we've had concepts to relate, both real and imagined. Our campfire stories of today can be traced back to a primitive world in which hunters regaled their tribes with tales of near misses with saber-toothed tigers and hair-raising encounters with woolly mammoths. The art of animation can also find its roots in these ancient times. As Roy E. Disney, former vice chairman of The Walt Disney Company, often points out, the prehistoric humans who created sequential paintings on cave walls were essentially the world's first animators, sharing their stories visually with the rest of their tribe. Humankind has always recognized the communicative power of words and pictures. Over time, people came to use both the written word and the painted image, employing each art on its own and in any number of combinations to share ideas, for business and pleasure, survival and diversion.

Once mere survival became less of an issue, our ancestors turned their attention and resources to the finer things in life, including the arts. By the time of Aristotle (384–322 B.C.E.), theater had become an integral part of civic life in Athens, which had one of the most advanced civilizations of its day. In fact, it was Aristotle in his *Poetics* who first codified the three-act structure that drives almost all commercial entertainment today. While the concepts and themes explored in theater would continue to evolve and expand over the centuries, the essential three-act structure itself survived into an age in which theatrical productions would be filmed and projected onto movie screens and beamed into television sets.

These days, movie audiences enter the theater with certain expectations, and a solid narrative with a distinct beginning, middle, and end is chief among them. For the most part, the typical movie audience wants to experience a complete, definitively ended story with accessible characters, situations, and themes, and a compelling narrative rife with conflict and the resulting drama and emotions that spring from it. That is what provides them with an escape from their everyday lives, which is what they want when they go to the movies.

> Since the beginning of mankind, the fable tellers have not only given us entertainment but a kind of wisdom, humor, and understanding that, like all true art, remains imperishable through the ages.
>
> —Walt Disney

## Mommy, Where Do Ideas Come From?: The Second Most Asked Question About Creation

Film is usually a storytelling medium, experimental and abstract works aside, so, in the movie industry, story ideas are the coin of the realm. To most people who live and work outside the industry, and to many of those trying to break in, screenwriting is the most mystifying and elusive of processes. One question commonly asked of writers in all mediums is, "Where do your ideas come from?" The short and over-simplified answer is that ideas can come from anywhere. The real trick lies in keeping the channel open and maintaining a running inventory of every item in every shipment. At some point your mind is going to have to play the role of "idea filter" and zero in on the ones you'd really like to pursue, but at most other times you can't afford to discriminate. Ideas can come from anywhere at any time, and they can slip into—and out of—your mind with alarming speed, so experienced writers train themselves to be there to meet them with open arms (and something to write them down upon) when they are kind enough to show up.

The development team at Walt Disney Feature Animation recognizes the elusive quality of good ideas and remains open to any and all potential stories. Some of the best Disney animated features are adaptations of beloved fairy tales, myths, and legends—*Snow White and the Seven Dwarfs*, *Cinderella*, *The Little Mermaid*, *Beauty and the Beast*—stories that were already very much a part of our collective culture when they were adapted into films. Classic literature, children's and adult, has also inspired a number of Disney's richest screen stories, including *101 Dalmatians*, *The Jungle Book*, *The Many Adventures of Winnie the Pooh*, *Oliver & Company* and *The Hunchback of Notre Dame*. History has proved to be fertile ground in both animation and live-action, yielding stories based on such figures as Mulan and King Arthur. And as Walt and his successors became more confident in their own storytelling prowess, they increasingly turned to the creation of original stories such as *Lady and the Tramp*, *The Lion King*, and *Lilo & Stitch*. Today Disney is casting an even wider net, inviting outside writers to come in and pitch their own ideas, something that has never been part of Disney's process in the past.

Disney's needs and processes may be unique to the company, but the Disney philosophy works just as well for the individual screenwriter. Source material surrounds you and it is filled with an endless supply of ideas for you to turn into stories. Fairy tales, myths, legends, and many classic works of literature have the advantage of being in the public domain, so if a compelling new approach to an old favorite is something that frees your creative spirit, go for it. Or let the *spirit* of the genre guide you in the creation of new fairy tales, modern myths, and legends of tomorrow, as George Lucas and the Wachowski brothers have done with the *Star Wars* saga and *The Matrix* trilogy, respectively. And what is humankind's collective history but one big, endless story made up of countless little ones? You can always find or create a little story set against the backdrop of a bigger, well-known one. That certainly worked out well for James Cameron when he told a tale of two fictional passengers sailing aboard a certain doomed ocean liner. You can even consider optioning or buying a property to adapt: books, magazine and newspaper articles—such as was the case with *Greyfriars Bobby* or *Remember the Titans*—or even the true story of someone you know, as long as their tale is compelling enough to share with the world. Even theme park attractions have provided fodder for fiction—thus, *Pirates of the Caribbean: The Curse of the Black Pearl.*

Many screenwriters, however, are interested in telling their own stories, presenting their unique vision of the world and its inhabitants. Hollywood is always looking for new stories or, at the very least, old stories told in new ways, and new voices to tell them.

There is no one correct course—for you or anyone else, including the "pros." The Oscar-winning screen-

> *I look for a story with heart. It should be a simple story with characters the audience really can care about. They've got to have a rooting interest.*
>
> —Walt Disney

writer William Goldman is widely considered to be a master adapter of famous books (*Harper* and *All the President's Men*), and yet it is one of his original stories, *The Princess Bride* (which he adapted from his own novel), that stands among his most enduring and popular works. Charlie Kaufman, on the other hand, is often—and correctly—hailed as one of the most inventive and wildly original screenwriters working today. In *Adaptation* he crafted an indisputably original story (and that's an understatement) to take the place of a problematic adaptation of Susan Orlean's *The Orchid Thief*, and received an Academy Award nomination for Best Adapted Screenplay. Look no further for smoking-gun proof that writers should always follow their muse, wherever it may lead them.

No matter what kind of story you ultimately choose to tell, the most important thing is to keep yourself open to *all* the possibilities and give yourself permission to go wherever the ideas and your own passions take you. That is one of the most important creative principles that the storytellers at Walt Disney Feature Animation have followed to build the rich and diverse body of work that defines their tradition and remains their legacy.

## Learning to Adapt ..............................

"The book was better." How many times have you heard that as you emerged from a theater showing the film adaptation of a book? Especially a film based on a book with lots of loyal fans, most of whom are quite vocal about the results—and are rarely happy with them. They feel the book was better because the film version just couldn't compare to the movie that played in their mind as they were reading. *Of course* they're going to prefer their own vision to anything Hollywood could possibly offer. What they often fail to consider is that literary fiction and film are two completely different mediums, with their own strengths, weaknesses, and creative requirements. They can never really be the same, nor should they try to be.

The best filmmakers focus on what is best for their movie, even if it means making alterations to the source material. After all, source material is just that—a source, an inspiration, a starting point—but once a book begins its long journey to film, it ceases to be a book. All of the creative content—story, setting, period, characters—must be viewed within the context of its new existence, its new reality as a blueprint for a film. Screenwriters and directors alike are wise to remember that and not remain slavish to something that no longer exists. The book will always be there for its fans, so feel free to start fresh and serve the story—the *screen* story.

## Fairy Tales, Myths, and Legends ...................

Walt Disney Feature Animation has always been known for its fairy tales. This was true in the days of *Snow White* and *Cinderella* and it is just as true in the age of *The Little Mermaid* and *Beauty and the Beast*. In fact, the fairy tale is usually the first thing that comes to mind when people think of Disney animation. As source material, fairy tales offer many advantages: they are full of ripe, dramatic situations that entertain and enlighten; they have unusual characters; and they offer satisfying solutions to the moral questions they pose.

These tales, originating centuries ago and constantly reinventing themselves throughout humankind's ever-changing cultural landscape, have many reasons in common for their appeal: they express the dreams of thousands of people; they represent, in an unadulterated way, the essence of human experience; and they address questions of purpose. One more thing they have in common is that none are ready for an immediate and unaltered translation into a motion picture. Walt, and later his successors, quickly discovered that they would have to cut beloved characters, create entire new subplots from whole cloth, and even add musical numbers to stories that in their original form do not include any references to singing or music. The creative liberties they took led audiences and critics alike to hail and sometimes deride the vast narrative differences in the Disney versions. But there was a method to Disney's alleged madness.

"Literary versions of old fairy tales are usually thin and briefly told," said Walt. "They must be expanded and embellished to meet the requirements of theater playing time, and the common enjoyment of all members of moviegoing families. The screen version must perceive and emphasize the basic moral intent and the values upon which every great fairy tale is founded. To these ends I have devoted my own best efforts and the talents of my organization, in full realization of our responsibility as a mass entertainer and especially our responsibility to our vast audience of children around the world."

Walt Disney had no problem tinkering with the classics when it came to their film adaptations. "From years of experience," he said, "I have learned what could legitimately be added to increase the thrills and delights of a fairy tale without violating the moral and meaning of the original. Audiences have confirmed this unmistakably. We define the heroines and heroes more vividly; add minor characters to help carry the story line; virtually create such immortal friends of the heroine as the Seven Dwarfs. Storywise, we sharpen the decisive triumph of good over evil with our valiant knights—the issues which represent our moral ideals. We do it in a romantic fashion, easily comprehended by children. In this respect, moving pictures are more potent than volumes of familiar words in books."

Walt managed to get away with his adaptation of familiar stories without too much complaint from critics and purists until he took on *Alice in Wonderland*, the first property with a devoted readership attached to it. During the development of *Alice*, Walt and his team tried to come up with ways to make the story work better as a film, including expanding the role of the White Knight to that of

> To captivate our varied and worldwide audience of all ages, the nature and treatment of the fairy tale, the legend, the myth have to be elementary, simple. Good and evil, the antagonists of all great drama in some guise, must be believably personalized. The moral ideas common to all humanity must be upheld. The victories must not be too easy. Strife to test valor is and always will be the basic ingredient of the animated tale, as of all screen entertainments.
>
> —Walt Disney

conquering hero. Lewis Carroll purists didn't think their beloved story needed a leading man. Having seen the liberties Walt took with his earlier adaptions of other classics, they set off a firestorm, bombarding him with angry letters and threats to boycott the film.

In this particular instance Walt relented and agreed to follow the book a bit more faithfully—and it shows. The resulting film is very episodic, with Alice encountering a variety of colorful characters as she drifts from one scene to the next. Although the film features some of Disney's finest character work and classic set pieces such as the Mad Tea Party, the lackluster whole can't possibly equal the sum of its manic parts. Walt promised himself and his staff that he would never take on such an untouchable classic ever again. He didn't keep that promise, of course, and by the time subsequent adaptations such as *Sleeping Beauty* and *The Jungle Book* were put into production, he had returned to his policy of putting the film first. That policy continues to this day and still garners both praise and criticism.

Ron Clements, co–writer-director of *The Little Mermaid*, *Aladdin*, *Hercules*, and *Treasure Planet*, often tells the story of being in Copenhagen for the European premiere of *Mermaid* and getting hit pretty hard by the press for the changes he and co–writer-director John Musker made to Hans Christian Andersen's story, "particularly changing his ending, where the mermaid had originally died. I started feeling so guilty that when I met the Queen of Denmark at the end of the premiere I apologized for what we had done to Andersen's story. Her reply was, 'Oh, he never knew how to end his stories anyway. Now it has a proper ending!' I know she was being a good diplomat, but it made me feel better.

"Later, when we were dealing with *Hercules*, we took a lot of heat as well, for changing Greek mythology. Our rationale was that the mythology was written over hundreds of years, was constantly reinvented, and was full of inconsistencies anyway."[3]

"[Ron and John] have tapped into popular culture," says producer Alice Dewey, who worked with them on *Hercules*, "which is part of what makes their movies really fun and accessible. There were people working on *Aladdin* who thought, 'Oooh, our movies are supposed to be timeless. What we're doing with the Genie and with anachronistic humor is very risky.' It was risky, but in their movies Ron and John take a high road and a low road at the same time, so there's plenty for everybody in the audience to enjoy."[4]

"The bottom line," Ron Clements concludes, "is that these films are *inspired* by their sources, they're not meant to be faithful adaptations. We use them as a jumping-off point. We try to be faithful to the essence of the material, not so much out of a sense of obligation, but because we figure there's a reason this stuff became so popular in the first place—and we don't want to lose that. We always hope we can somehow make it better, at least for the medium we're tackling. If we were too inhibited, it would be almost impossible to do anything."[5]

This philosophy extended to filmmakers who chose to adapt the legend of Fa Mulan. Just as the Greek myths evolved and changed throughout their history, so the fable of the legendary Chinese warrior had remade itself through the years of telling. "When I discovered the broad history of the legend—the many different versions of the story in China and across Asia," director Barry Cook recalls, "I began to see that there was freedom to enhance and change. I felt very relieved. I realized it wasn't a historical document. We weren't dealing with something so literal that we couldn't enhance it. That knowledge was liberating. That's when we could let our imagination kick in."[6]

## A Classic Example ·······························

*Beauty and the Beast* was the first animated feature to be nominated for an Academy Award in the Best Picture category, which until that point had been the exclusive domain of live-action films. (*Snow White and the Seven Dwarfs* had received one full-size Honorary Oscar—and seven little ones—in 1939.) The film was produced at the height of Disney's second golden age of animation, joining *The Little Mermaid* as a modern classic, with *Aladdin* and *The Lion King* waiting in the wings. It is a film that perfectly exemplifies that notion of a magical alchemy, with every single element, from story and characters to music and song, playing its part to perfection. And with all those strong, individual elements working so harmoniously together, *Beauty and the Beast* came as close to perfection as any film during Walt's time. It is also a masterpiece of adaptation.

Like many of the fairy tales upon which some of the most beloved Disney animated features are based, *Beauty and the Beast* was not tailor-made for the big screen. The original literary versions of the story were too complex, and required substantial alterations to make the narrative compelling to a modern audience. Paper-thin characters with often inexplicable motivations and a second act that basically consisted of two of those characters having dinner night after night meant that the production team, consisting of directors Gary Trousdale and Kirk Wise, screenwriter Linda Woolverton, and producer Don Hahn had their work cut out for them.

Beauty and the Beast–themed stories have existed in folklore since ancient times. The story of a young girl paired with a hideous beast was a favorite of the mid-eighteenth-century French court and was first published in a form similar to the story we know today by Madame Gabrielle de Villeneuve in 1740. This was followed by the most widely known version, by Madame Marie-Jeanne le Prince de Beaumont, which was printed in France in 1756 and in England in 1783. The fairy tale has the titular Beauty's father spending the night in an enchanted castle after getting lost in a storm. He happens upon a beautiful rose garden and decides to cut a branch to take home as a present for his favorite daughter. The master of the castle, a horrific beast, suddenly appears and rails at the old man for violating the one thing he loves in life: his roses. The Beast insists that the trespasser must pay for this capital offense with his life, or with one of his daughters. The man returns home, explains his predicament to his family, and Beauty selflessly agrees to take her father's place in the Beast's castle.

Beauty takes up residence in the Beast's castle, and must listen to a new marriage proposal from him each night at dinner.

> I think we have made the fairy tale fashionable again. That is, our own blend of theatrical mythology. The fairy tale of film—created with the magic of animation—is the mode equivalent of the great parables of the Middle Ages. Creation is the word. Not adaptation. Not version. We can translate the ancient fairy tale into its mode equivalent without losing the lovely patina and the savor of its once-upon-a-time quality. I think our films have brought new adult respect for the fairy tale. We have proved that the age-old kind of entertainment based on the classic fairy tale recognizes no young, no old.
>
> —Walt Disney

She turns him down, although she does come to see the goodness buried deep within him as the days and dinners go by. A turning point comes when Beauty peers into the Beast's magic mirror (every good fairy tale has to have one!) and discovers that her father has fallen ill.

The Beast allows Beauty to return home, warning her that he will die within a week if she fails to return to him. She makes it home to her father, but her selfish sisters delay her return to the Beast until it is almost too late. Upon returning to the castle, Beauty finds the Beast near death, a sight that prompts her to declare her love for him. The power of her love transforms him into a handsome prince, and Beauty and the Beast—you guessed it—live happily ever after.

After an early draft was deemed too dark and melodramatic, the Feature Animation brass pointed out that songs had given *The Little Mermaid* its light touch, and lyricist Howard Ashman and composer Alan Menken joined the *Beauty and the Beast* team. As was expected, the Ashman–Menken influence extended well beyond music and song, and the two musical-theater veterans once again helped point the way to some key story solutions.

"Howard was really good at plot," *Beauty and the Beast* screenwriter Linda Woolverton recalls. "He always said he was 'the simplicity police.' When things started getting too complicated and 'plotty,' he'd say, 'These movies have to be very simple, they must move simply.' He would always make us stop going off on tangents and come back to the purity of the source, the emotion of the source. Howard told us that every single scene, not just the ones you'd expect, but every one should have an umbrella of emotion over it, whether it's warmth or terror or love or drama or even comedy. Every single scene."[7]

Two of the central problems with the original story material were Beauty herself (and with half the title devoted to her character, that is indeed a problem) and an intimate dinner party sequence that ran the length of the second act. Linda Woolverton dedicated herself to the creation of a new kind of Disney heroine, while Ashman and Menken brought two sets of fresh eyes to the overall story.

"It's very difficult to take the originals and convert them into a story that works for a modern audience," says Woolverton. "You have to consider what kids are like now in terms of sophistication; you have to make sure that your themes are strong, that people can relate to the characters, that the story isn't sexist."[8]

After reading and watching every imaginable interpretation of *Beauty and the Beast*, including Jean Cocteau's 1934 film classic and the late 1980s cult hit television series, Woolverton finally arrived at her version of the female lead, Belle. In the original fairy tale in particular, Beauty was little more than a pawn in a game controlled by either the Beast or her father, her actions largely dictated by blind devotion to these two male figures. Woolverton knew that such a delicate and passive "little woman" might have played just fine in the 1950s, but would be virtually unacceptable in the waning years of the twentieth century.

Picking up where the trail blazed by *The Little Mermaid* left off, Woolverton set about crafting a character smarter and more determined than any previous Disney heroine, including the feisty Ariel. Belle has ideas and dreams of her own, as shown by her relentless reading about the real and imagined worlds around her. *She* will decide whom to marry (and when), and none of the dim and dull men in her quiet village fits the bill in her estimation. Belle definitely isn't your grandfather's—or even your father's—Disney heroine.

"Belle is a strong, smart, courageous woman," Woolverton affirms. "She sacrifices herself for her father. There are great themes of passionate love in the story, almost operatic themes. She's a Disney heroine who reads books. We've never seen that before."[9]

The product of Woolverton's resolve is a thoroughly modern woman who happens to live in eighteenth-century France. She is a strong and

> Storytellers for all time have taken core story material and adapted and changed it for their audience, their era, and their point of view. Giambattista, the Brothers Grimm, Charles Perrault, Hans Christian Andersen, every storyteller throughout time. To say that we 'Disneyfy' something as a pejorative in terms of adapting a narrative is to reveal one's complete näiveté about the process and history of storytelling.[10]
>
> —former Walt Disney Feature Animation president Thomas Schumacher

independent character who turns the notion of a traditional Disney princess on its ear. The story finally has a Beauty every bit as relevant and powerful as the mighty Beast who shares the title. In the process of creating the screenplay, Belle became a positive role model for the new generations of young girls who would embrace this character and this story just as those in Walt's time had connected with Snow White and Cinderella.

As for the problematic second act, Howard Ashman turned to some of the background characters and story devices from the fairy tale to reconceive it. First, he suggested that the Beast's household staff, which suffers from the same curse that transformed their master, be more than the mere inanimate objects of an earlier draft. At his urging, they were turned into the decidedly animated "enchanted objects" that audiences would come to know and love: a candelabrum, a mantle clock, a teapot, and a chipped teacup, among hundreds of others. This troupe of supporting characters provides much-needed comic relief and also helps to bring out different aspects of both Belle and the Beast's characters, a vital function of any good supporting player. And, perhaps most important of all, Lumiere, Cogsworth, Mrs. Potts, Chip, and the rest of the newly animated household staff turn one of the original tale's interminable dinners into the show-stopping production number, "Be Our Guest."

Two other supporting characters from the original fairy tale were also given expanded roles that would help keep act two charging forward into act three: one of the Beast's beloved roses and that ubiquitous magic mirror. The dying rose puts a time limit on the Beast's quest to find someone who will love him. The magic mirror provides a link to the outside world, one that will show Belle the jeopardy in which she has placed her father by declining the marriage proposal of her boorish suitor, Gaston. Instead of falling ill, as in the fairy tale, her father gets carted off to a lunatic asylum thanks to Gaston's scheming. That provides the motivation for Belle to leave the Beast's castle and go to her father's aid. The magic mirror also reveals a mob of advancing villagers, prompting the heart-broken Beast to say, "Let them come," thus setting up a battle royal in act three.

The result of these innovative adaptations is a compelling new interpretation of a classic story that not only resonates with modern audiences but also keeps them glued to their seats for the length of a feature film, something that a blindly faithful interpretation of the fairy tale could not do. *Beauty and the Beast* remains true to the *spirit* of the tale, retaining many of its characters, plot devices, and themes, while establishing its own distinct identity. That delicate balance ensures that an age-old story, told in a brand new way, may endure for generations to come. And *that* is the real art of adaptation.

# American Originals ••••••••••••••••••••••••••••••

One of the words most often used to describe Walt Disney is "original," and yet the majority of the studio's animated features have been based not on original screenplays but on adaptations of fairy tales, myths, legends, and classic children's books. Even *Dumbo*, which is widely believed to be an original Disney creation, is based on a story by Helen Aberson and Harold Pearl. Ultimately, *adaptation* and *original* aren't entirely fair designations, considering how wildly inventive the Disney animated features can be. The liberties Walt took with his adaptations often led them so far from the source material that the average filmgoer came to think of the properties as original Walt Disney creations. Ask just about anyone about *Pinocchio*, *Bambi*, *Cinderella*, and *Peter Pan*, and, rightly or wrongly, they will instantly think of the Disney versions. So, as you can imagine, the line between original and adaptation can get pretty blurry at The Walt Disney Studios.

None of this is to say that certain pieces of source material don't allow more latitude than others, because they do. No one decried the "Disney versions" of *The Aristocats* or *The Fox and the Hound*, because far fewer people were passionate about or even familiar with the original works on which those films were based.

Walt's first truly "original" story came a full eighteen years after *Snow White and the Seven Dwarfs*. *Lady and the Tramp* was released in 1955, the same year in which Disneyland opened its doors. The project actually dated back to 1937, when Walt began developing a story about a sweet and demure cocker spaniel.

In 1943, Walt happened across an unpublished short story entitled "Happy Dan, the Whistling Dog," by Ward Greene, who was an editor at King Features, the company that syndicated Disney's comic strips. Happy Dan was a free spirit, a charming rogue who answered only to himself.

"Your dog and my dog have got to get together," Walt told Greene, who immediately agreed and cobbled together a new story, "Happy Dan, the Whistling Dog, and Miss Patsy, the Beautiful Spaniel." In many ways, it was Walt's first commissioned screen story. Although Walt was pleased with the result, which was sort of a *When Happy Met Patsy* romance, it would be another ten years before the film went into production under its new title, *Lady and the Tramp*.

This original production was a refreshing change of pace for Walt. "We were free to develop the story as we saw fit, which is not the case when you work on a classic," he said. "Then you must adhere rigidly to the sequences conceived by the author, which are familiar to your audience. Here, as the characters came to life and the scenes took shape, we were able to alter, embellish, eliminate, and change to improve the material." Although it can be argued that Walt rarely "adhered rigidly" to his source material (when he adhered to it at all), it's clear from this statement that he actually felt liberated after the attacks he had endured for "tampering" with classics such as *Alice in Wonderland* and *Peter Pan* in the early 1950s.

The ultimate proof that *Lady and the Tramp* was a true Disney original came when RKO sales executives and even author Ward Greene himself fought Walt over the title, likely concerned about the use of the word *tramp* (RKO Radio Pictures was distributing Disney films at the time). Walt wouldn't even consider changing the title of a story that he had developed from word one: "That's what it's about— a lady and a tramp," he argued.

*Lady and the Tramp* took its rightful place among Walt Disney Feature Animation's most enduring classics, so it could be considered somewhat odd that Walt immediately went back to adaptations and stuck with them until his death. *Sleeping Beauty*, *101 Dalmatians*, *The Sword in the Stone*, and *The Jungle Book* were all based on existing properties. It would be almost forty years after *Lady and the Tramp* before Disney produced an animated feature based on an original story—a little film called *The Lion King*.

Most if not all original stories start with a classic *What if . . . ?* question. The right *What if . . . ?* question can lead to an interesting situation or premise, which, in turn, can lead you to an interesting story. The issues of who, what, where, when, why, and how work themselves out later when you begin to shape the story and the characters that will drive it. Take a closer look at some of your own favorite films, and you will likely find that they can be traced back to a simple question or notion.

*What if we could bring back the dinosaurs?* for example, became the *Jurassic Park* franchise. *What if a young boy woke up one morning to find himself in a man's body?* became *Big* (and several other similarly plotted movies that year). *What if the result of a dangerous alien genetic experiment escaped from prison, stole a space vehicle, and crash-landed on Hawaii, where he was adopted by an Elvis Presley–loving misfit girl who believes a fish controls the weather?* You never know where a *What if . . . ?* will take you.

## Stitching Together a Story ••••••••••••••••••••••••

The origin of *Lilo & Stitch* dates back to the mid-1980s, when the film's co-writer and co-director, a young artist named Chris Sanders, drew a sketch of a peculiar little creature with a grinning, almost Cheshire Cat–like face, a gaping mouth, large, batlike ears, and six legs. This was to be the main character in a children's picture book that Sanders was considering but ultimately abandoned. The sketch was placed in a drawer. The main reason that the image wasn't lost forever is that, as an early experiment in photography, Sanders took a picture of his desktop in 1985, upon which the sketch happened to be laying. That fateful photo and the sketch itself were destined to become very important.

Fast-forward twelve years, to October 1997, when Feature Animation held something of a summit meeting on Michael Eisner's family farm in rural Vermont. The guests included Roy and Patty Disney, Feature Animation president Thomas Schumacher, producer Don Hahn, and Pixar's John Lasseter. Some of the studio's most successful directors were present as well, including the *Beauty and the Beast* team of Gary Trousdale and Kirk Wise, and *The Lion King* co-director Roger Allers.

The studio wanted to evaluate where Disney Animation had come over the previous ten years, and where it might go in the next ten. Many of the participants felt that Disney's animated features had grown too elaborate, too complicated, and, in some cases, a little too slick and polished. This also meant that they were getting too expensive. Bigger didn't always mean better, and the team worried that in the process of becoming big budget "event films," Disney's animated features were in danger of losing some of their charm.

Chris Sanders recalls the summit. "One of the questions that came up was, 'Can we make a smaller, riskier, more quirky film?' When they said, 'Okay, do you have a story like this?' I went back to this old story I had about this little monster that lived in this big forest. It was modified to a little alien marooned on earth, and that was the start of the movie."[11]

When Sanders dusted off his strange little creature, all he had was a "broken little character and about thirty percent of a structure to hang him on."[12] He met with then Feature Animation president Thomas Schumacher at a sushi restaurant in the Swan Hotel at Walt Disney World to pitch his burgeoning story. Schumacher had the sudden brainstorm to maroon the creature in the human world since, in his words, "The animal world is already, in a sense, alien to us."[13] That one small creative suggestion immediately unlocked all sorts of story possibilities in Sanders's mind. His "little monster," soon to be known as Stitch, was about to meet a fellow misfit: a young Hawaiian girl and diehard Elvis fan named Lilo.

As the story began to take shape, quirkiness, served with a side of originality, was the order of the day. Stitch wouldn't be a strange species of animal with no past, lost in a vast forest, but a dangerous genetic experiment from a distant alien world, and a criminal to boot. Not only would he be marooned in the human world but in one of its most beautiful and idyllic corners: Hawaii.

Sanders and co–writer-director Dean DeBlois' originality streak continued with their other title character, Lilo, who was born almost fifteen years after that first little sketch of what would become Stitch. Far from being the picture-perfect Disney heroine, Lilo would look and act much more like a "real" person. With her penchant for antisocial behavior, Lilo was decidedly different from the very beginning (but then again she would have to be, in order to go toe-to-toe with Stitch for ninety minutes). As if these offbeat qualities weren't more than enough to guarantee them one of the most unique creations in Disney history, Sanders and DeBlois also made little Lilo one serious Elvis aficionado.

When Lilo met Stitch the fireworks really began, and the Feature Animation team knew they had something different on their hands, if nothing else. Roy Disney's reaction—"Lilo & Stitch? What's a Lilo? And what the heck's a Stitch?"[14] —was typical in the early days. In the "Play it safe, or it's your job" world of Hollywood, you can imagine the initial responses Sanders and DeBlois got to their pitch: "Well, it's about this alien genetic experiment and intergalactic criminal who crash-lands in Hawaii and meets a little girl who loves Elvis and adopts him because she thinks he's a dog."[15] As Austin Powers's nemesis Dr. Evil would say, "Rrri-i-ight."

Feature Animation was committed to their quest to try something different. They believed in this strange little story and, more to the point, they believed in Chris Sanders and Dean DeBlois. As Lilo and Stitch made their journey from concept sketch to storyboard to pencil test to story reel to final animation, the entire studio began to realize they had something special on their hands. Although the project would benefit from the collaborative approach common to all filmmaking and Disney animation in particular, much of the originality of *Lilo & Stitch* can be attributed to the studio's faith and trust in the singular voices of two artists with very specific points of view. In many ways, the past and future of Disney storytelling collided in the production of one very special movie, merging the creative chaos of collaboration with the determination and specific vision of the individual. The very best of both approaches was evident on the screen, and audiences around the world responded in kind. *Lilo & Stitch* became Disney's biggest traditionally animated hit in years.

Adaptations of one sort or another may be (and remain) the most common type of story told at Feature Animation, but there will always be room for stories that exist only in a screenwriter's imagination, waiting to be set free.

An original idea can come from anywhere, and the creative development team at Walt Disney Feature Animation team looks everywhere. "We concentrate a lot on story and writers. Part of our job is to try and come up with new ideas for stories," says Mary-Jane Ruggels, Vice President of Creative Affairs at Walt Disney Feature Animation. "We look at fairy tales and legends. We look at the classics; we look at Shakespeare. We think about countries or animals that haven't been explored. We're doing an animal-caper movie right now because we haven't done that before, and we're doing a mystery movie because we've always been interested in the mystery genre. We'd love to do something in the Latin world, so we've been looking at Mexican and Central American legends. We were looking to do something based in Ireland for a long time and had a couple of things in development. We didn't end up doing one of those, but it does show what a great source countries and regions are for brainstorming fresh approaches to storytelling.

> *There are fashions in reading, even in thinking. You don't have to follow them unless you want to. On the other hand, watch out! Don't stick too closely to your favorite subject. That would keep you from adventuring into other fields. It's silly to build a wall around your interests.*
>
> —Walt Disney

We attack the search for new ideas from many different angles. It's not only, what fairy tale or classic haven't we told yet. It can also be, what setting is fresh, what animal is fresh, what genre is fresh? When you've told as many stories as we have, it's hard to find something that feels different."[16]

Walt Disney Feature Animation now approaches the development process in much the same way as any live-action studio in Hollywood. The creative team still looks at fairy tales, books, animals, and the folklore of many countries, but they are also increasingly open to inviting outside writers and directors to come in and pitch their own ideas for original stories and characters. That's an exciting new prospect for filmmakers everywhere, who just may be working on the world's next *Lady and the Tramp*, *The Lion King*, or *Lilo & Stitch*.

## Timeliness versus Timelessness ••••••••••••••••••

One of the main reasons Disney animated features have weathered the test of time so well is that the clear majority of them are considered *timeless* as opposed to *timely*. Timeless films often have a fantasy, natural, or even period setting, and, for the most part, don't say or portray anything that might tie them to the time in which they were made. Timely films, on the other hand, usually have a contemporary setting and don't shy away from portraying contemporary values, allowing their characters to use current slang, and making pop cultural references that could easily be out of date within months.

These are not hard-and-fast rules in animation or live-action, however. *It's a Wonderful Life* and *Home Alone* are both considered timeless holiday classics (and relentlessly referred to as such). Both featured contemporary settings and themes upon their release in 1946 and 1990, respectively, which does not appear to be an issue with the people who continue to watch and enjoy them every year.

There are also plenty of films that were revolutionary at the time of their release, including *Guess Who's Coming to Dinner*, *Easy Rider*, *Network*, and *Wall Street*, and that still are and always will be considered classics even though they are hopelessly dated in many ways. Not even science fiction is immune to this syndrome. Try watching *Star Wars: A New Hope*, which takes place a long time ago in a galaxy far, far away, without commenting on the blown-dry hairstyles of Mark Hamill and Harrison Ford, both of which are straight out of the 1970s.

Although such artistic and commercial successes as *101 Dalmatians* and *Lilo & Stitch* have featured contemporary settings, many timely films have not fared nearly as well. The most timeless animated features are set in a fantasyland or the natural world, enabling them to work as well for subsequent generations as for their first audience. That's why *Bambi* works just as well today as it did during its initial release in 1942, and why *The Little Mermaid* will be just as relevant to the audiences of 2039 as it was to those of 1989.

*Fantasy, if it's really convincing, can't become dated for the simple reason that it represents a flight into a dimension that lies beyond the reach of time. In this new dimension, whatever it is, nothing corrodes or gets run down at the heel, or gets to look ridiculous like, say, the celluloid collar or the bustle. And nobody gets any older.*
—Walt Disney

Although much of a film's timeless quality can be attributed to its setting and lack of specific time period, some of it has more to do with the story's approach to character and humor. Walt in particular was careful to stay away from catchphrases and any cultural references or other such elements that could immediately date a film, just for the short-term payoff of a cheap laugh or two. But if the humor derives organically from the unique situation in which a well-defined character finds him- or herself, the film has a much better chance at remaining accessible to audiences for decades to come.

One glaring exception only proves the rule. When the voice talent signed on to play the Genie in *Aladdin*, co-directors Ron Clements and John Musker knew they were going to have to stay openminded to take full advantage of the free-associating comic genius in their midst. Sure enough, the Genie fires off thoroughly contemporary references and celebrity impersonations throughout the film—and it works. Why? Because there is a solid story explanation for the anachronisms that not only gives the filmmakers permission to leave them in but enables the audience to enjoy them without wondering, "Whoa, where did *that* come from?" They know, because they have been repeatedly shown and told, that the Genie is a magical being, a free spirit (in every sense of the term) who knows no boundaries of space or time. He can go wherever he wants, whenever he wants, and consort with whomever he wants. So when the Genie calls for a "group hug" or launches into impressions of Woody Allen and Jack Nicholson, the other characters are justifiably mystified and the audience is understandably delighted. But screenwriters beware—not everyone or every film can get away with something like that. *Aladdin* could and did because it had a once-in-a-generation talent and two gifted writer-directors to guide him.

Another major contributor to the effect of timelessness is the Disney approach to character design, especially in films set in the animal world. The animals in many of the animated features are very naturalistic and not overly anthropomorphized. For the most part, the characters look like real wild animals in a natural setting. They are not dressed up as people. This is critical to the allegorical quality of films such as *Bambi* and *Brother Bear*. How can we believe what the films have to say if we can't believe, on some level, that its characters are as real as we are? The Disney approach to animal characters also makes the films more akin to fairy tales and Aesop's fables, which have also withstood the tests of time and changing culture in their quests to illuminate different aspects of the human condition. This is why *The Lion King* is already considered an undisputed timeless classic, while *The Aristocats* and *Robin Hood* somehow feel mired in their time (the 1970s) in spite of their onscreen settings of turn-of-the-century Paris and medieval Sherwood Forest. Filmmakers need to think twice about what they're trying to say and how convincing they want to be when they say it before they make an alley cat or a grizzly bear put on a pair of pants.

*Brother Bear* is the most recent example of this particular timeliness versus timelessness debate in action. One early version of the screenplay was essentially "*King Lear* with bears." The story revolved around an elderly bear and his three daughters, and was inspired by Shakespeare's play in much the same way that *Hamlet* influenced *The Lion King*. In that version, the animals were very anthropomorphized, wearing clothes and slamming cave doors in fits of teen angst. The creative team saw the early warning signs and steered their project away from what they referred to as "*Robin Hood* territory." Taking their cue from *Bambi* and *The Lion King*, they decided their film would star much more naturalistic animals in an attempt to achieve the timeless quality that marks so many of the Disney classics.

Striving for a timeless quality didn't mean that the *Brother Bear* filmmakers couldn't have as much fun with their characters as Ron Clements and John Musker had with their Genie. The filmmakers knew they needed a pair of characters to perform a number of important story functions and provide comic relief. The pair of Canadian moose, Rutt and Tuke, voiced by Dave Thomas and Rick Moranis, respectively, might appear at first glance to be little more than a comic device that runs the risk of pulling viewers out of the world unfolding onscreen. But the characters do not date the film, thanks to the organic way in which they are worked into the overall story. Since the film is set in a mythical North American wilderness that incorporates elements of the American Pacific Northwest, Alaska, and Canada, a pair of dim-witted Canadian moose seems like a perfect fit. And it works.

The entire audience can appreciate them as funny characters well integrated into the story; younger viewers laugh at their intellectually challenged antics; and adults derive added value from their fondness for these two great comic actors. The filmmakers put their desire for a timeless story first and then found ways to build on it to create both comic and narrative possibilities that work for different segments of the audience.

## Tell Me a Story ................................

Settling on a great idea can demand blood, sweat, toil, and tears from a storyteller, but the hardest work is yet to come. Now that you have an idea of what kind of story you'd like to tell, you have to, well, tell it. I'm sure you've met any number of people who have claimed, "I'm an idea person," or "I have a lot of great ideas, I just don't know how to write them down." But you obviously want to develop your ideas into more than just a passing thought, and in order to do that, you have to get them down on paper. Ideas are a dime a dozen; you must have a way to articulate them properly and share them with others.

It's not easy. And it shouldn't be easy. "If it were easy, everyone would do it," as your parents undoubtedly told you about any number of things that seemed far too difficult to consider pursuing. And it is difficult. If you've been truly inspired, however, there's a good chance your muse will stick around long enough to help you do the heavy lifting.

*"Nothing in a lifetime of picture making has been more exciting and personally satisfactory than delving into the wonders, the mysteries, the magnificent commonplaces of life around us and passing them on via the screen."*

Walt Disney

# Perspiration

*"The way to get started is to quit talking and begin doing."*
Walt Disney

• • • • • • • • • • • • • • • • • • • • • • • • • • • • • • • • • • • • • • • • • • •

O nce you have a great idea, one that's just going to burn a hole in your brain until you share it with the world, everything else should just fall into place, right? Hardly. Not even here in the Magic Kingdom. A great idea and a great script—or any script, actually—are two completely different things, and one is easier to come by than the other. You could pick up today's newspaper and find a dozen stories that would make solid movies. As important as great ideas are, they really are a dime a dozen unless you have the ability and determination to articulate them properly. That's what those upcoming 90 to 120 blank pages are all about. That's what separates the men and women from the mice, even at The Walt Disney Studios. To paraphrase Walt, you have to stop thinking and start writing. You have to transform your ideas into a narrative. You have to be able to *tell me a story*.

## First Things First . . . Now What Comes First? • • • • • •

Okay, so you're ready to get to work and start writing. Now what? You may have a lot of disparate creative elements floating around in your head, but what comes first? The story (and its trickier inner structure, the plot)? The characters? An overriding theme? Ask this question of a dozen different animation writers and directors and you will get a dozen different answers, and all of them would be right.

"Nothing comes 'first,' " says Don Hahn, producer of *Beauty and the Beast*, *The Lion King*, and *The Hunchback of Notre Dame*, among others. "That would be like somebody saying, 'Well, you have to write the lyrics first and then write the music.' Well, no, some people want to write the music first. Or it's like cooking. Some people say 'Well, you have to blend these ingredients first and then you add that.' That's where the magic or mystery comes in. Every film-maker will do it differently."[17]

Some writers start by structuring the plot, expanding upon their initial inspiration. Was it a classic *What if . . . ?* question that triggered the idea? *What if* a god were forced to become mortal? *What if* a girl took her father's place in battle? *What if* a boy found a map to the greatest treasure in the universe? More questions will then logically follow: *Who* is the main character? *How* and *what* do they need to do to attain their goal? *Where* and *when* does the action happen? *Why* are they doing it in the first place? As you explore and answer these questions, you create a solid foundation upon which you can build your story.

Other storytellers begin with a character and create a situation through which they can best explore that character. *Lilo & Stitch*, for example, began with a simple sketch of Stitch, who wasn't even Stitch at the time—or an alien genetic experiment, for that matter. Little Lilo, a lush Hawaiian island setting, and Elvis didn't come into play until fifteen years later. Each one of those elements offered Chris Sanders a different way to explore a different aspect of the funny little creature that had sprung out of his mind and onto a sketchpad so many years earlier.

Don't ever underestimate the power of memorable characters, however. Some of the most successful franchises in movie history, from James Bond to Indiana Jones to Harry Potter, are almost entirely character-driven. The individual adventures themselves aren't nearly as important to most moviegoers as the chance to see their favorite characters again and spend some more time with them. There are still pitfalls associated with this—the filmmakers in question would do well to keep a close eye on their narratives, as hundreds of surly critics will be quick to point out, but you get the idea.

While many writers—novelists, playwrights, and screenwriters alike—swear up and down that theme emerges from story, there are storytellers who have a theme in mind and then build the right story through which to share it. There is no one right way to do this, remember? Far from emerging *from* the story, the deceptively simple theme "Be yourself" was consciously reinforced in *Aladdin* throughout its development. And "Don't judge a book by its cover" has been a key theme of *Beauty and the Beast* since its incarnation as a fairy tale.

And there can be more than one theme. Aaron Blaise and Bob Walker, the co-directors of *Brother Bear*, feel that one of their strongest themes, "You can't become a man until you learn to make decisions based on love," guided their story from its early days. But another theme emerged as the story took shape: "You may look at your 'enemy' in a different way after seeing the world through his eyes." You never want to allow the tail to wag the dog (or the bear, as it were)—that is, a film must avoid coming off as preachy—but the right theme can be a powerful inspiration. It will then be up to you to meet your theme's challenge and follow through with just the right story and characters to share it with your audience.

These three elements of story—situation, or plot, characters, and theme—are the dominant forces in the creation of Disney's animated features, and most other pieces of filmed entertainment, for that matter. The studio's unwavering focus on story and character, in particular, can be traced straight back to Walt Disney's earliest short cartoons.

## The Circle of Strife: From Script to Storyboard to Script and Back Again..........................

There's no way around this, so we might as well just deal with it up front: the script as we know and fear it has never been king at Walt Disney Feature Animation. For decades, scripts for the animated features didn't even exist, at least not on paper. But they were there. Walt Disney just happened to carry them around in his head, that's all. As with anything else, we need to take a look at the past in order to understand the present and prepare for the future. In the beginning there was Walt, and, more often than not, that was enough.

Walt knew what stories he wanted to tell and he knew how he wanted them to be told. He possessed a singular vision that powered and guided an entire motion picture studio and the hundreds of creative people who worked there. That does not, however, mean that he did everything, nor does it mean that he did it alone. Walt collaborated with his story artists, animators, and directors just as surely as artists from hundreds of disciplines work together to produce the animated and live-action films of today. The key difference lies in the foundation upon which the films are built now. Today the script is the common denominator for everyone working on a production. During Disney's golden age of animation, it was Walt. He literally *was* the script.

Former vice-chairman of Feature Animation and Walt's nephew Roy E. Disney, has his own story to tell. "It was a Sunday night. I was upstairs in bed with the chicken pox, and Walt and Lilly came over to have dinner with my mother and dad. Walt came upstairs to say hi to me. They were right in the midst of story development of *Pinocchio* at the time. He said, 'Well, we're making this new film, let me tell you a little about it.' He must have gotten carried away, because he sat there on the edge of my bed and acted out the entire story of Pinocchio, from start to finish. He did all of the characters. And the joke that I've always told about him was that when I finally saw the movie, it was nowhere near as good as the story Walt told me in my bedroom that night!"[18]

"On *Alice in Wonderland*," says Joe Grant, co-writer of such films as *Dumbo* and *Fantasia*, "he *was* the script. We didn't write anything. He'd go from room to room, recite the same story, and everybody would add something. The end result of that process was *Snow White*, *Pinocchio*—almost every picture we did."[19]

Just as he acted out the story of *Snow White* for his animators one fateful night on a studio soundstage, just as he told his nephew the story of *Pinocchio*, Walt shared his stories—and his vision—with the collaborators that would bring them to life onscreen. He accomplished this with a steady stream of story meetings that took place throughout the life of a production, particularly during its early days.

In these story meetings, Walt built his films sequence by sequence, beat by beat, sketch by sketch. Nothing escaped his attention. He addressed every aspect of story development and construction, from the tiniest pieces of dialogue to character design to major plot points. Detailed written transcripts of the story meetings were made, many of which came to resemble a standard film script. Sketches were drawn and pinned to the wall from the beginning of the process—the first "storyboards." Lines of dialogue and passages of action and description were tacked beneath the story sketches. The "script," such as it was, emerged from this chaotic mélange of words and pictures.

"When Walt held a meeting," said Assistant Director Jane Sinclair Kinney, "it was mandatory that everybody understood what he meant. So they always had a secretary who took all the notes. She was obliged to record them verbatim, particularly for Walt. And when these meetings were over with, carbons were made for each one of these people, and of course the reason was that nobody was to misunderstand Walt, because what he said had to be done. He also had a chronic cough," she added, "but he always seemed to get that cough when he was bored, particularly if something bothered him in the picture, so that was recorded in the notes."[20]

The transcripts provided a running account of Walt's thoughts on any given subject, along with the opinions and ideas of his artists. This process made the films' production a fairly fluid one. Throughout production, the animators revised the storyboards much as a screenwriter would crank out new drafts of a script. Sketches were pulled off the storyboards and replaced with new ones. Dialogue was changed as the characters evolved. Entire sequences were added, cut, or moved around, turning the story into something of an elaborate jigsaw puzzle until Walt saw the picture he wanted. It was never too late to make something better, either. If a sequence wasn't working, even after it had been animated, it could always be sent back to the story room.

Marc Davis was one of Walt Disney's original "Nine Old Men" of animation and a key animator on many of the first Disney golden-age films. "This man could tell a story so well," said Marc, "and if you had the problem of having to animate this you thought, 'My God, could I in any way animate this as well as I have seen him do it?' And he could pantomime these things. He'd get up and he could do every one of these characters, and you believed him."[21]

When Michael Eisner became chairman and chief executive officer of Disney in 1984, he quickly immersed himself in the art and business of animation. After spending two decades in live-action films and television, Eisner was uncomfortable with Feature Animation's scriptless approach to filmmaking. "It's okay to do it that way if you've got a guy verbalizing the script. Walt Disney could do that. He carried everything in his head,"[22] Eisner said during that period. "I couldn't follow it. I'd go down there and they'd go through the storyboards, and you'd go through one storyboard and then they'd bring in another storyboard, and you'd sit there for hours, and I couldn't remember what was on the first storyboard, and it was a very hard process for me to deal with. I'm used to dealing with scripts. And I was a little critical of some of our animated films that had been done since Walt died, because I thought they had great scenes, but were just a lot of scenes put together. Sometimes the arc of the story didn't follow the way I was used to thinking about stories or what I had learned in school about the construction of a story. I kept thinking about this, and every time I asked how it was done in the past I'd hear about Walt and how he would jump up and down and he'd go back and forth between things. And then Roy Disney told me a story about how Walt sat on his bed when Roy was sick and told him the entire story of *Pinocchio*, and I finally discovered that they did have a script . . . and the script was in Walt Disney's head. Well, we didn't have a Walt Disney, and therefore we didn't have a single mind tracking the entire movie. We had a committee of minds and that was the problem. Now we do scripts."[23]

Feature Animation's new way of doing business was not terribly far removed from the traditional process. The main difference was that each film would now employ actual screenwriters—sometimes the directors themselves—to guide (or, in some cases, at least to track) the story's evolution. This would help ensure that everyone, from the directors to the story artists to the composer and lyricist, was on the same page, literally and figuratively.

For the most part, it was still the directors who provided the guiding vision for the movies they wanted to make. In the early days of a project, the director led their production team, including the screenwriters, in the creation of a story outline board, which consisted of small strips of paper pinned to a storyboard that described, beat by beat, the plot of a film. It is not very different from a traditional screenwriter's outline, but more people are involved and the collaborative process begins much earlier.

The motion picture in general, and the animated film in particular, is a visual medium; for that reason, story points can often be more effectively made in pictures rather than words. That is where the story artists come in. Their job is to take script pages from the screenwriter and visualize them in storyboards. "Basically you're putting a written idea into visual terms and seeing how you can make it play emotionally and finding the places to express the humor that's latent in the characters,"[25] says Roger Allers. This leads to a sometimes grueling process of give-and-take between the collaborators, with changes made in both mediums in order to tell the strongest possible story.

"The screenwriter–story team relationship is hopefully one that encourages brainstorming, debating, and finally breakthroughs," says Brian Pimental, head of story for *Tarzan*. "The process is rarely smooth. You fight to get all these different things onto the script page. And then when it's time for storyboarding, you find other problems that you hadn't seen before because you were just dealing with words and now you're dealing with images as well. There are moments of disagreement, but you need that. It's sort of a checks-and-balances approach to getting the very best you can up on the screen."[26]

Writers must often go back and revise their scripts based on the way the story artists have boarded a sequence and communicated an idea visually. Story artists, on the other hand, sometimes need to be reigned in when their visual flights of fancy lead them too far astray from the story. The directors, like Walt before them, are there to maintain this delicate balance.

"The writers of *Hercules* knew that the directors birthed the project and we were there to nurture and guide it—kind of like godparents," says writer Irene Mecchi. "Working with everybody was kind of like a jazz improvisation—you'd throw an idea to the group, and who knew where it would go? It got really wild at times. It was based on trust—or total insanity."[27]

*Brother Bear* producer Chuck Williams makes an apt comparison between animated films and live theatrical productions. "The storyboarding process is a lot like rehearsing a play," Williams says, "but, in our case, 'opening night' is the start of actual production. Everyone on the production team wants to get each sequence as 'right' as they possibly can before the expensive and labor-intensive animation process begins. So by cutting the storyboards with dialogue, music, and sound effects, it gives us a chance to throw it up on the big screen and make changes—much like the rehearsal period of a play. The big difference is, of course, the characters, in particular, immediately take on new dimensions as soon as the voice talent gets involved, and, even more to the point, when the animators themselves begin to bring them to life."[28]

"Most simply put," says Francis Glebas, story artist on *Pocahontas*, "story artists take what the writers do and translate it into picture language. Then the writers see our images and that inspires them to write even better stuff. It goes back and forth in a truly collaborative process."[29]

Today the evolution continues, with Feature Animation making a concerted effort to lock in the script before proceeding even to the storyboard stage. In this way the development of animated features grows to be more like that of live-action films. The goal is to minimize the number of changes made between the stages of scripting, storyboarding, and animation, with a more solid foundation in place before a project moves from development into production. Combined with Feature Animation's new willingness to take pitches from outside sources, this makes it more conceivable for a screenwriter to walk into The Walt Disney Studios with a full script that has not already been assigned to a director or a team of story artists. That's a long way from one man orally telling a story that would be faithfully visualized and realized by hundreds of artists.

## The Outline: A Writer's Personal Storyboard · · · · · · ·

In many ways, Walt talked and acted his films into existence. So, in a sense, by talking he actually was doing. But even in Walt's process there came a point when he had to quit talking so his animators could begin doing, and take over from the story men and sketch artists. For the screenwriters of today, that means taking your ideas, which you have probably thought about and talked about to death, and cobbling them into written outlines, treatments, and, eventually, scripts.

In creating an outline, the screenwriter is able to block out every beat, scene, sequence, and act. You can examine your story as a whole or break it down into its most individual components. The outline, in many ways, is like a writer's storyboard. Think about it: setting the visual element aside, your outline really isn't much different from Walt's storyboards, at least in terms of story content. This is particularly true when your scenes are put down on 3x5 cards and

On every animated movie, things are free-form and loose in the beginning. As the story develops, ideas begin to funnel down and need to go hand-in-hand with the movie everyone decides we're going to make. The early stuff is never lost, though, because you get to pick and choose from your wildest or most conventional ideas. The story always leads the charge.[30]

—Ralph Zondag, story artist, Pocahontas

laid out on the dining room table, or on the floor, or tacked up to—you guessed it—a board.

The use of the 3x5-card format really allows you to see your entire story at a glance, much as Walt could see an entire film unfold before him on his storyboards. You can add and cut scenes, color code them to indicate beats or action to orchestrate a rhythm or establish a flow, and move them around until you are happy with the structure of your story. This allows you to test different directions and can reveal potential trouble spots before you've committed too much to paper. It allows you to test out different directions and will reveal potential trouble spots. It's much easier to throw out a scene when it's a couple of sentences on a 3x5 card instead of five pages of script. If you can work out the majority of your story problems in an outline, and then expand your narrative into a more detailed treatment, writing the actual script will be a much easier part of your process. Not easy, mind you—writing a script is rarely a day at Disneyland—but easier if much of the difficult and tedious story construction work has already been done.

## Plotting a Course......................................

*There are three things that make a Disney animated film so special: story, story, and story.*[31]

—Roy E. Disney

Ideas and stories are two distinctly different animals, and just because you may possess the former doesn't mean you are guaranteed the latter. Your great idea may offer only the barest suggestion of a full story, but the average moviegoer isn't going to spend hard-earned money to see a suggestion. It's going to take a lot of perspiration to turn inspiration into culmination: a finished and complete screenplay. On many of Disney's animated features, the writers and directors discovered that they had their work cut out for them even when the ideas they were starting with were ostensibly complete stories.

Anyone at The Walt Disney Studios can tell you how hard it is to create a ninety-minute movie from the fairy tales, myths, and legends that have inspired so many of the animated features. An equal number of storytellers will counter that it is every bit as difficult to fill those ninety minutes when you have entire novels from which to work. That could mean the several hundred, densely packed pages of Victor Hugo's *The Hunchback of Notre Dame*, or a whole series of books such as Edgar Rice Burroughs's *Tarzan* stories. In those instances, perhaps there is almost too much story, and the challenge is to find one gem of a narrative to commit to film. Or maybe the story is so complex, abstract, or nontraditionally structured that some serious alterations need to be made to create the more linear and family-friendly structure of an animated feature.

So who has it tougher? The answer is that they all do. *We* all do. And that is because it is no small feat for any screenwriter to fill ninety minutes to two hours, or, more to the point, 90 to 120 pages. Those pages need to be filled with a compelling story that transports an audience to another world and introduces them to memorable characters with whom they want to spend that precious time. That calls for a screenplay that will make readers want to turn the page, desperate to discover what happens next, a good screenplay that will make a good movie sure to keep viewers glued to their seats.

Disney's stories all follow a traditional three-act structure, the template for almost all commercial

Story is such an elusive monster. At moments, it seems so incredibly clear and within my grasp; at other times, intangible and distant.[32]
—From director Kevin Lima's *Tarzan* diar

(meaning Hollywood) films. In its essence, the paradigm, or model, is deceptively simple. An old screenwriting proverb puts it this way: in act one, you get your character up a tree; in act two, you throw rocks at him for an hour or so; and in act three, you get him down. In other words, the first act is all about setting up your characters and story, establishing a central action that needs to be achieved or overcome, and setting opposing forces into motion. The second act consists of a series of escalating complications that prevent the protagonist from getting what he or she wants relative to that central action. In the third act, the hero overcomes the greatest and most serious of those complications to achieve their goal, whether it's kissing the princess, saving 101 Dalmatian puppies or finding Treasure Planet.

The "plotting" of the story beats (those moments when a story takes a new direction, emotional growth occurs, or a piece of the mystery's puzzle is revealed) takes your audience from point A to point B to point C—and from act one to act two to act three—and results in, appropriately enough, the plot. Some of these beats help set up the story in act one and wrap up the story in act three. Others have an even greater impact and provide major turning points in the story, such as those at the end of the first and second acts.

The first major story beat is a catalyst commonly known as the *inciting incident*. This is a development that sets up a problem or goal for the protagonist and motivates (and often forces) them to take action. The Magic Mirror informs the Queen that Snow White is, in fact, the fairest in the land, leading the villainess to conspire to do away with the young princess. Belle's father gets lost in the woods, prompting her to go look for him. Mulan's ailing father is conscripted, triggering her decision to take his place in battle. The plot of every story can be traced back to one incident that sets everything in motion and places the protagonist in the necessary position to make choices and take one action instead of another.

The two biggest story beats following the inciting incident are the act one and act two *curtains* (also known as *plot points*, *turning points*, or *rising action*) both of which give the story a nice shot of adrenaline and send it spiraling off in a new and unexpected direction. *The Lion King* offers solid examples of story beats that very clearly define the beginning of the film's second and third acts and raise the stakes for its hero. In act one we've met the current lion king, Mufasa, and his spirited son, Simba, who is destined to follow in his father's paw prints. But, unbeknownst to father and son, Simba's uncle Scar has designs on the throne. The death of Mufasa (for which Scar is responsible) and Simba's resulting guilt (he thinks it is his fault) force the lion cub into exile and the beginning of act two. There he turns his back on his family and embraces the *hakuna matata* philosophy of his new friends Timon and Pumbaa, renouncing the ambition expressed in his earlier song, "I Just Can't Wait to Be King."

Simba's later decision to embrace his destiny and fight for what is rightfully his, which he makes after he is reunited with his childhood friend Nala and learns of Scar's destruction of his homeland, is another major reversal that leads him back to the Pride Lands and into act three for a final confrontation with Scar. These two emotional moments mark the most important plot developments in the film, and provide a strong framework for the rest of the story.

As was stated earlier, act two is that hour your character spends trapped in a tree deflecting flying rocks, or the various obstacles that create conflict in your story. For your sake and the audience's, those rocks had better be nice and

With story, you have to take baby steps to your goal. It can be pretty discouraging. Part of our dilemma has been trying to integrate humor and emotion. In the beginning, it's hard to know how it will all fit together.[33]

—Bonnie Arnold
producer, *Tarzan*

big, come fast and hard, and hit their mark every once in a while. If not, your audience just sits there watching someone lounge in a tree for an hour—and you can imagine how exciting that is.

Just as there is no shortage of rocks to hurl at that character in the tree, there is a vast and diverse array of obstacles with which to confront your characters. Some of those obstacles are physical; others take emotional or psychological forms. The composition of the obstacles derives naturally from your main plot, subplots, and the primary and secondary conflicts your characters face throughout the story. Aladdin must survive a series of escalating physical conflicts with Jafar while struggling internally with the truth of his identity and the acceptance of self that will ultimately win him Jasmine's hand. Mulan engages in the ultimate physical conflict: war with the Huns. At the same time, she plays a psychological game of gender deception with her compatriots and yearns to reveal the girl she sees in her reflection throughout the journey. The combination of such escalating conflicts should bring your characters to physical, mental, and emotional breaking points as act two draws to a close.

Why can second acts be such a challenge? "Beginning and endings have closed ends to them," Chris Sanders suggests, "The second act doesn't have closed ends—both ends are open. It's up to you how long it's going to run, so one of the questions of the second act is: how big is the journey? And it's always a journey. Take *Beauty and the Beast*, that was a journey of the heart. So, how long is it going to take for her to come around and fall in love with this guy? Is it going to take too long? Or not long enough? In a way, the second act is infinite with what you can do. If you were crazy, you could make a ten-hour movie about a character who came around so slowly that nobody would watch it!"[34]

Act three brings us the film's climax, in which the protagonist takes an action that steers the story toward final resolution and answers the central question: will our hero get what he wants? The climax is the point of highest tension in the story, a bigger turning point than either of the two act curtains. Prince Phillip finally defeats the dragon Maleficent and goes to wake his sleeping beauty. Cinderella finds herself locked in by her stepmother while her sisters try on the telltale glass slipper. She escapes that trap, only to watch Lady Tremaine destroy the evidence. But Cinderella has one last card to play—she has the other slipper. She and the Prince can then live happily ever after.

Although the entire battle sequence in the castle at the end of *Beauty and the Beast* is climactic, the climax itself takes place when Belle declares her love for the dying Beast, which lifts the curse and makes him human again. Belle's declaration answers the central question of whether or not she can learn to love a beast. In the process, she realizes her dream of escaping her little town, and Beast is freed from his dreaded curse. In *The Lion King*, Simba finally faces and defeats Scar, taking his rightful place as king of the jungle. What Simba is really facing is himself and the past he has left behind; he is avenging his father's death and exorcising the demons of guilt that he had wrongly attached to it.

The action of the climax should feel irreversible, true, and right, leaving the audience feeling that everything is as it should be in the world of the story as the narrative comes to an end. That doesn't necessarily mean it has to be a *happy* ending either; it just means that the audience should be left feeling that the story could not have ended in any other way.

## Zero to Hero: The Hero's Journey and the Magic of Mythic Structure ···············

"Zero to Hero" may be the name of a musical number from *Hercules*, but it is also a telling summation of the elements of mythic structure that have become increasingly prevalent in film storytelling. In an age when the *Star Wars* and *Lord of the Rings* films have brought mythic structure and archetypal characters out of the classroom and into the mainstream, it is worth noting that these story concepts and narrative devices have also had a significant influence on Disney's animated features. Many Disney films, especially the more recent ones, offer a variation on the Hero's Journey, a mythic paradigm mostly defined in the works of Lord Raglan (*The Hero: A Study in Tradition, Myth and Drama*, 1936) and Joseph Campbell (*The Hero of a Thousand Faces*, 1949).

The theme of the Hero's Journey appeared in the myths of cultures around the world in ancient times, and has been woven into the fabric of popular storytelling ever since. The hero's story employs time-honored devices (the reluctant young hero's seeking the counsel of an older mentor figure, or a journey into the underworld) and well-defined characters, or archetypes (such as the trickster, who also often provides comic relief, or the shadow, who mirrors the hero in a negative way), that the audience immediately recognizes and relates to, even if on a subconscious level. These stories have become such an integral part of human culture that we instinctively respond to them whenever we see or hear any of their elements.

The hero paradigm works particularly well in films because it closely aligns with the three-act structure, which, as we have seen, guides the construction of most mainstream screen stories. As the hero's story begins, a

[The Lion King] *has very much of the Hero's Journey structure to it, whereby a character is catapulted into growing up by some catastrophic incident in his life. Then he has to go conquer many things, get over many hurdles, seek the wisdom of the wise man, and return triumphant to his kingdom.*[35]

—Don Hahn,
producer of *The Lion King*

situation arises that calls for the protagonist to leave the comfort and safety of home and embark on a journey into an extraordinary world fraught with adventure, danger, risk, and uncertainty. In this new world, the hero must overcome a series of increasingly dangerous challenges and antagonistic forces to achieve, acquire, or learn something of incalculable value, a reward. Our protagonist must then elude or defeat any remaining opposition in order to bring this reward back home, forever changing the hero and his or her people.

Act one takes place in the ordinary world. Our protagonist, a seemingly ordinary person (or animal), receives a call to adventure; some new condition, development, or event changes or threatens to change the status quo of the hero's world, calling on him or her to act. Hercules discovers that he was adopted by mortals and he is really a god. Jim Hawkins inherits a treasure map from the dying Billy Bones. The hero typically refuses this call at first. After careful consideration, and usually after consultation with some sort of mentor figure, the hero accepts the call and strikes out on a journey into the extraordinary world. Guided by the ultimate mentor, Merlin, the young Wart embarks on a heroic quest for the Sword in the Stone. The mouse Bernard, a meek and mild janitor, reluctantly agrees to join Miss Bianca on the daring rescue of a young kidnapped girl, Penny, to become *The Rescuers*. The event that finally convinces or forces the hero to accept the call is generally the turning point that brings the curtain down on act one. The death of Bambi's mother irreversibly places the young prince on the path to adulthood. Shere Khan's return to the jungle ends Mowgli's tranquil life with Bagheera and forces the man cub to go into hiding with Baloo in *The Jungle Book*.

Act two consists of the long and perilous journey into the extraordinary world. Our hero, along with any allies brought along or picked up along the way, descends ever deeper into this foreign environment, where the group braves a set of increasingly demanding mental, emotional, and physical challenges such as the daunting combination of threats faced by Aladdin and Mulan, as we saw earlier. At some point, the protagonists meet up with their enemy and engage in conflicts that also escalate in severity until the hero comes face-to-face with the main antagonist. Although Taran survives a series of encounters with lowly minions and the more formidable undead soldiers, he must ultimately face the evil Horned King for control of the Black Cauldron. Honest John and Stromboli both fail to put Pinocchio on the chopping block, but little woodenhead must rescue Geppetto from no less an adversary than Monstro the whale before he can become a real boy. In most stories, the hero must battle this ultimate villain for the reward. The hero somehow manages to earn the reward—though the villain is not necessarily defeated—and must escape with it (and his or her life) back to the ordinary world. The winning of this reward and the new sets of circumstances and consequences it creates bring the second act to a close and sets up the climax to come in act three. Aladdin discovers that Jasmine will indeed love and accept him for who he is, but both of them still have Jafar to contend with before they can live happily ever after. Mulan is revealed to be a daughter of China, not a son, but there is still that small matter of war with the Huns. And the adult Simba finally comes to grips with the truth of his father's death, but a deadly confrontation with Scar still awaits him back in the Pride Lands.

Act three chronicles the hero's return trip to the ordinary world and his or her own people, now armed with the knowledge, experience, or object that was the goal in the first place, such as the noble stand an enlightened Pocahontas makes for the previously unknowable John Smith, or a vindicated Simba's return to the Pride Lands. The villain has not taken kindly to the hero's victory at the end of act two, and dispatches all the forces of evil to finish off our hero once and for all. The protagonist, realizing that winning the battle does not necessarily mean winning the war, must marshal the forces of good to preserve act two's hard-earned reward at any cost. Prince Eric finally learns the truth about Ariel—and loves her anyway—but the sea witch Ursula has won command of the sea from King Triton and is not about to let them live happily ever after without a fight—and it's a big one. The final battle between hero and villain occurs toward the end of act three and is typically the climax of the entire story. Once the protagonist has scored this final victory, he or she can safely return to the ordinary world, forever changed by the experiences in the extraordinary world. The remainder of the story deals with this resolution and, possibly, the transformation of the ordinary world that is brought about by the hero's return with the hard-earned reward.

The Hero's Journey is very clearly exemplified in *Aladdin*. We meet our hero as a street rat living by his wits on the wrong side of the tracks in Agrabah. This is his ordinary world. Aladdin's call to adventure comes through a fateful encounter with the evil vizier, Jafar, who is in search of a magic lamp that will enable him to become a powerful sorcerer and take over the kingdom. Aladdin crosses the threshold into an extraordinary world when he descends into the Cave of Wonders in search of the lamp.

His journey in this special realm continues when he releases the Genie of the lamp, who grants him those infamous three wishes. Aladdin, desperate to make a permanent escape from his ordinary life as a street rat, uses the Genie's powers to transform himself into the dashing Prince Ali, a royal suitor worthy of the hand of the fair Princess Jasmine. She falls for the false prince, seemingly making him a permanent part of the extraordinary world to which he has longed to escape.

Jafar, meanwhile, carries on with his plot to overthrow the Sultan. Jasmine only discovers Aladdin's true identity as the vizier takes over her father's kingdom by magical force, which compels our young hero to rise to the occasion without the use of the Genie's magic or a false identity. In the end, it is Aladdin, not Prince Ali, who vanquishes Jafar and wins Jasmine's heart, transforming himself and his entire world in the process. In addition to the more obvious reward of Princess Jasmine's love, Aladdin is enriched by the realization that the people of both worlds would see him as the "diamond in the rough" that he really is, if only he would learn to be himself.

One of the most recent and compelling examples of the Hero's Journey at work is *Brother Bear*. The film tells the story of Kenai, an impetuous young Native American eager to become a man. When his eldest brother, Sitka, is killed by a bear, Kenai swears revenge and sets out after the monster over the objections of his older brother, Denahi. He finds and kills the bear, but the Great Spirits—his fallen brother, Sitka, in particular—transform Kenai into that which he hates most, a bear, in order to teach him about the destructive nature of vengeance and the healing power of love. Even in death, Sitka knows that only when Kenai learns to let love guide his actions can he ever truly hope to become a man.

Against his will, Kenai leaves the ordinary (and human) world of his tribe, and all he thinks he knows, for an adventure in the extraordinary, natural world of his enemy, bears. The difference between the two worlds is even better defined in this film than in *Aladdin*, because Kenai is actually made a physical part of the extraordinary world in order to make a journey and earn his reward. The protagonist literally becomes his own antagonist—the transformation gives Kenai a first-hand look at his own hatred and vengeance. His brother, Denahi, thinks that Kenai has been killed, not transformed, and tracks him with the intent to avenge the second brother he believes to have fallen to a bear. Perhaps not even Joseph Campbell could have foreseen such a collision of two worlds, the human and the animal.

The story's conclusion is also distinctive, in that the hero makes a conscious decision to stay in the extraordinary world, rather than return to his ordinary world. Armed with his reward and its transforming, healing power, Kenai has finally learned to let love guide his actions in his relationship with the bear cub Koda. As his journey draws to a close, Kenai realizes that he had first to become a bear in order to become a man, but he still chooses to remain a bear.

You can apply elements of the Hero's Journey to your story to give it some of the added weight and timelessness that are hallmarks of world culture's most enduring tales. You don't have to (and probably shouldn't) follow the paradigm to the letter. Some of the steps of the journey may be taken out of order, combined, or even deleted entirely. Luke Skywalker's call to adventure, for example, comes directly from Obi-Wan Kenobi, a mentor figure with whom he meets for most of act one before accepting the call. In *The Sword in the Stone*, the future King Arthur's call to adventure is placed by the original mentor archetype, Merlin. Aladdin's call to adventure actually comes from the villain, when Jafar recruits him to retrieve the lamp from the Cave of Wonders. Characters can and very often do wear the masks of more than one archetype, making them even more unpredictable and thus interesting than they otherwise might have been. Aladdin's Genie is clearly a mentor figure, but he also assumes the role of trickster, providing comic relief while guiding our young hero.

Adding, subtracting, mixing, and matching these plot developments and characterizations can ultimately help prevent your story from becoming too formulaic. Playing with the paradigm is a way for you to make your tale feel familiar yet original to the audience, all at the same time. Unless you are dead set on crafting the next *Usual Suspects* or *Memento*, you shouldn't be afraid of that "familiar" aspect of the Hero's Journey, either. A dash—or even a healthy dose—of familiarity is something for which you should strive in creating mainstream commercial entertainment. Audiences have proven time and again that they respond to stories that don't stray too far from what they're comfortable with, yet surprise them in the process. That's why some sequels work and others don't. If you can give the audience the best of what they liked the first time around *and* take things in a slightly different direction in the process (*The Godfather* films are a good example), they will respond. If you offer nothing more than a complete rehash or pale imitation of the original, they will stay away in droves.

Your best bet is to use the paradigm as more of a measuring stick than a road map. Check in with it every once in a while to chart your progress rather than follow it to the letter. If you find that your story generally seems to reflect the spirit of the paradigm, then you are much more likely to have crafted a tale that has the richness, resonance, and relevance of the Hero's Journey stories that have endured for millennia.

## Songs Can Move You . . . and Your Story**••••••••••••**

*We should set a new pattern, a new way to use music.*
*Weave it into the story so somebody just doesn't burst*
*into song.*

—Walt Disney

The Disney tradition of animated musicals dates back to *Snow White and the Seven Dwarfs*, when Walt and his team did indeed "set a new pattern." Unlike many Broadway shows and live-action musicals of the 1930s and 1940s, the early animated films didn't feature showy production numbers that imposed on the action and stopped the narrative dead in its tracks. To the contrary, the songs emerged organically from the story, defining character and advancing the plot while entertaining the audience. Walt rarely included a song for its own sake; every song had to play a role within the whole film, just as the characters did.

"Music has always had a prominent part in all our products," said Walt. "So much so, in fact, that I cannot think of the pictorial story without thinking about the complementary music that will fulfill it.

Often the musical themes come first, suggesting a way of treatment. This was the case with the Tchaikovsky music for *Sleeping Beauty*, which finally formulated our presentation of the classic. I have had no formal music training. But by long experience and by strong personal leaning in the selection of musical themes, original or adapted, we were guided to wide audience acceptance. Credit for the memorable songs and scores must, of course, go the brilliant composers and musicians who have been associated with me through the years."

The Silly Symphony *Three Little Pigs* was a critical and financial success for Walt, but it also taught him the value of telling a story through song. When he began work on *Snow White*, he kept this in mind. Of course, he wanted the songs to stand on their own merits, but his first concern was to make sure that each song helped to tell the story.

Almost all of Walt's animated features were full-blown musicals, a tradition from which he began to deviate in the early 1960s with films such as *101 Dalmatians* and *The Sword in the Stone*. While these films include a catchy song here and there, they can hardly be considered musicals in the classic sense. By the time the studio released *The Jungle Book* in 1967, the songs had become more like flashy showcases for such star vocal talent as Phil Harris and Louis Prima than the valuable narrative tools they had once been. This less ambitious approach to music and song continued until 1989, when *The Little Mermaid* re-established The Walt Disney Studios as one of the foremost producer of musicals, in Hollywood, on Broadway, and everywhere else.

Music and song have both continued to play everexpanding roles in the animated features. Some of the films are traditional musicals, such as *Beauty and the Beast*, *The Lion King*, *Pocahontas*, and *The Hunchback of Notre Dame*. Others use songs to accent or narrate the action, even if the characters themselves aren't doing much of the singing, as in *Tarzan*, *The Emperor's New Groove*, and *Brother Bear*.

Since the studio rediscovered the sheer storytelling power of what is essentially cinematic musical theater, a veritable "cast of songs" has emerged. Each of these "performers" has its own distinct part to play in the telling of a screen story. Many of them are direct descendants of numbers that appeared in Walt's films, and others reflect the strong influence of the stage musical and the artists who came to Disney from that discipline, including Howard Ashman, Alan Menken, Glenn Slater, Stephen Schwartz, and Tim Rice. Some songs correspond to types that fulfill crucial functions, such as introducing characters, delivering potentially tiresome exposition, or advancing the plot in ways that dialogue never could. Each of these song types frequently coincides with a key story beat in a film's overall structure. Other songs are more consciously designed with pure entertainment value in mind, yet even in those colorful showstoppers there is a lot more going on than meets the eye (and the ear).

"The music is a major element with *Beauty and the Beast* and *The Little Mermaid*," says Don Hahn. "Bringing Broadway musicals back into our films was a very fresh idea at the time. If you look at the Disney movies that are the most memorable, there's always a strong and different musical voice. Sometimes it's the Genie in a Las Vegas setting or Dumbo's mom singing to her little boy from a prison cage—these are key moments. Our 'Circle of Life' sequence has a very strong attachment to music. The next jump was using someone like Elton John. Nobody had really used rock stars to write musicals before—not with any success. It makes me laugh when people talk about how *Chicago* brought back the musical—we've been doing it for years now. It's an important emotional storytelling device."[37]

The "anthem" is a powerful song that often comes to symbolize the entire film and the themes for which it stands. When audiences hear the anthem, they automatically think of the film, so closely do the two relate to one another. It is generally a serious-minded piece that deals with sometimes weighty subject matter, most typically in act one. A musical presentation makes this kind of content much clearer and palatable to a broad audience, particularly younger moviegoers. Even a lighthearted film such as *Hercules* can have something important to say, and the anthem ("Go the Distance") enables the film to say it much more effectively and memorably than even the most impassioned piece of dialogue.

In *The Lion King*, the epic anthem "Circle of Life" effectively summarizes what the entire story is about in the film's opening minutes. It speaks of the natural order of things and a sacred connection between all living creatures, thematic elements that will have a strong bearing on the main plot and Simba's heroic journey from lion cub to lion king. At the same time, it introduces a number of the main characters and presents their unique place in the world in which the film takes place—all before we see the film's opening title card. "We completely threw out a dialogue scene at the opening of the movie—just completely threw it out," reveals co-director Rob Minkoff. "We said, let's just go with the music."[38]

The anthem of *Pocahontas*—the film in general and the character in particular—is the Oscar-winning "Colors of the Wind." The piece sets up the symbiotic relationship Pocahontas and her people enjoy with the earth, and simultaneously reveals how different their point of view is from that of the more materialistic colonists. Not only does the anthem define the character of Pocahontas, but it also helps portray the wind itself as an invisible yet tangible manifestation of this delicate and sacred natural world of which she is such an inseparable part.

"Ideally, a musical number comes out of a scene or situation," says James Pentecost, producer of *Pocahontas*. "But this song was written before anything else. 'Colors of the Wind' set the tone of the movie and defined the character of Pocahontas. Once Alan [Menken] and Stephen [Schwartz] wrote that song, we knew what the film was about."[39]

Act one is also the usual home of what has come to be known as the "I want" song, in which our hero or heroine sings of their hopes, dreams, and what they want most out of life. This is a tradition that can be traced back to Snow White's musical expression of hope in "I'm Wishing." Since these *are* Disney animated features we're talking about, the audience can reasonably expect their heroes to get what they want and live happily ever after. They know that the joy is going to lie in the journey itself. The "I want" number sets up that journey, lets the audience know what it's in for during the next ninety minutes, and gives them something to root for. Ariel's longing to be "Part of Your World," Mulan's "Reflection" of who she hopes to be, and Simba's impatience when he "Just Can't Wait to be King" ask the central questions that need to be answered before the end credits roll.

In *The Hunchback of Notre Dame*, Quasimodo dreams and sings about spending just one day "Out There" in the world beyond his bell tower. The manipulative Frollo has convinced Quasi that the streets of Paris would be a scary and dangerous place for him, and that no one outside the walls of Notre Dame could ever accept such a hideous creature. This fills Quasimodo with such a powerful yearning that it can best—and perhaps only—be expressed through music and song. The fact that the audience gets to share in this dream upon meeting Quasimodo makes it all the more moving and powerful for them when he ultimately realizes his dream.

The "I want" song in *Beauty and the Beast*, "Belle," serves several purposes, introducing the audience to the character of the same name while painting a picture of life in her quiet little town. We also get a pretty good idea of what the rest of the village thinks about Belle, her strange preoccupation with reading, and her ambitious dreams. In other words, there's a lot more going on in this song than a pretty girl singing about petty frivolities. The "I want" portion, where she shares her hopes and dreams musically, happens in a reprise when Belle is alone. The reprise reinforces and refines the character's motivations, as we also hear in the reprises of "Part of Your World" and "One Jump Ahead," for example.

Some songs are simply considered "pure entertainment," and the filmmakers don't make any bones about that. These segments come closest to the lavish Broadway production numbers of old, entertainment for entertainment's sake. If they don't do anything more for the narrative than elicit smiles from the audience, that's fine with even the most disciplined of Disney storytellers. That is rarely the case, however, because story is seldom abandoned entirely. Even the songs included ostensibly for their pure entertainment value in some way keep up the narrative momentum that has been established up to that point.

Take "Under the Sea" from *The Little Mermaid*, for instance, the first Disney song to win an Academy Award since "Chim Chim Cheree" in 1964's *Mary Poppins*. It's a full-blown production number that puts almost any live-action counterpart to shame, a visual tour-de-force and a musical testament to the power of magical alchemy. It is also Sebastian's counterpoint to Ariel's "I want" song, "Part of Your World," which sets up the central question of the movie. Sebastian and all his undersea friends may be singing and dancing and having a good time, but this elaborate effort is still a direct attempt to dissuade Ariel from pursuing her ultimate desire. This makes "Under the Sea" one of those act two obstacles we looked at earlier; and makes a song that appears to be purely entertaining a significant story point in disguise.

What would a Disney animated feature be without the "love song"? Romance has always been one of the primary ingredients in the Disney films, and music is one of the most effective ways to express it, as in the Academy Award winners "Beauty and the Beast" and "A Whole New World." Sometimes the love song overlaps slightly with the "I want" song, as in "Once Upon a Dream" from *Sleeping Beauty*, only to be reprised as the love song at the film's conclusion. In other stories it is a veritable "love anthem" that symbolizes the eternal connection between two characters, such as "So This Is Love" in *Cinderella* and the Oscar winner "You'll Be in My Heart" from *Tarzan*.

One of the most powerful recent examples of the love song is the Academy Award–winning "Can You Feel the Love Tonight?" from *The Lion King*. The film's composer, Elton John, had always wanted to write the quintessential Disney love song. In fact, it was one of his primary motivations for signing on to the film to begin with. "Elton told us that one thing that had attracted him to our project was the Disney tradition of great love songs," says Roger Allers, co-director of *The Lion King*, "and he knew he'd written a strong love song that fit right in with the animation. He was sure it could be made to express the two lions' feelings for each other far better than dialogue could. He was right, of course. In the end Tim [Rice] made some adjustments to the lyrics and everything fell into place."[40] This piece accompanies the pivotal and poignant moment in which Simba and his childhood sweetheart, Nala, finally connect.

The filmmakers, however, did not want to present their love song in a traditional Disney way. They were looking to avoid any kind of clichéd magic moment between their two romantic leads, and didn't want Simba and Nala to sing the song to each other. To that end, they proposed that Simba's brothers in exile, Timon and Pumbaa, perform the piece in a more ironic way, one that would convey their disgust over their pal's rekindled romance with his former girl. This would also make the important story point that they didn't want to lose the friend they had "raised" since he was a lion cub.

That suggestion didn't go over too well with Sir Elton, who wrote the number with every intention of creating just such a magical Disney moment. The composer compromised with his directors. He wrote a new opening verse for Timon and Pumbaa, one that would make the point that they weren't crazy about losing their pal to a woman. From this comedic opening the piece transitions into a heartfelt duet sung off screen—and not by Simba and Nala—to underscore this romantic reunion effectively. The filmmakers avoided their hackneyed romantic convention, and Elton John did indeed get his magical and musical Disney moment.

The bad guys need their moment in the sun too, of course, and they get it with the aptly named "villain song." Much like the antagonists themselves, their songs come in different shades and varying degrees of villainy. Some are simply musical celebrations of the subjects themselves and their nefarious accomplishments, such as "Ratigan" in *The Great Mouse Detective* and "Gaston" in *Beauty and the Beast*. They introduce the characters to the audience, giving viewers a clear picture of who these rogues really are and the pain and suffering they're capable of inflicting on our heroes. "Our goal was to write a song that, if you listened only to the music, would sound buoyant and harmless," says lyricist Stephen Schwartz on "Mine, Mine, Mine," the villain song from *Pocahontas*, "but if you listened to the words, you would realize that they are talking gleefully about destroying the entire countryside."[41]

Other villain songs play a more active role in the plot. In *The Little Mermaid*'s "Poor Unfortunate Souls," for example, Ursula spells out the conditions of her deal to make Ariel human for three days, taking the little mermaid's voice in exchange in the process. Once again, the filmmakers used a song to introduce a major turning point in the story, in this case a devil's bargain that factors into the villain's plot against the hero. And still others are nothing less than an all-out call to arms, such as the dark anthem Scar sings to his legion of hyena loyalists in "Be Prepared" from *The Lion King*. If the "I want" song introduces the protagonist and helps set up the ultimate goals and objectives of their journey, the villain song is often its direct counterpoint. This song establishes the antagonist, who will try to stop the hero from getting what they want, and, in many cases, spells out how they plan to pull it off and why they feel so strongly about it.

Disney films also employ music and a song to set up basic story elements and avoid the deadly slowness of endless expository material. They can also help transport characters from point A to point B, which, on a hero's journey, is often a key moment in which the hero acquires the skills needed to win the battle. Like that proverbial spoonful of sugar, such sequences go down much easier when set against a musical backdrop.

The smooth delivery of lengthy but necessary exposition is one of the most complicated tricks of the writer's trade, and can be enhanced by a little musical sleight-of-hand. *Hercules* has a lot of background to cover (the titular character's Mount Olympus origins) and utilizes a literal Greek chorus to give the audience "The Gospel Truth" about their hero. "The Bells of Notre Dame" ring out with the backstory of Quasimodo, and "Two Worlds" are explored as Tarzan's shipwrecked parents add a distinctly Victorian touch to the ultimate tree house.

A good melody can help a character get through any routine chore or exercise, whether it's cleaning the house, as in Snow White's tuneful suggestion to "Whistle While You Work" or marching from boot camp to the Imperial City, when Mulan learns about "A Girl Worth Fighting For." The passage through adolescence can pass much more lyrically, as in "Son of Man" from *Tarzan*, or lackadaisically, as in "Hakuna Matata" from *The Lion King*, as our heroes quickly and merrily eat, drink, and sing their way through Simba's teen years.

Characters often need a little basic training before they can embark on their Hero's Journey, and an inspirational—and motivational—song can help commit them to their cause. In these songs, a mentor figure often makes an important musical counterpoint that strengthens the protagonist's development or the story's theme while our hero is learning the ropes. Philoctetes expresses his desire (and motivation) for "One Last Hope" as Hercules gains the skills to go from zero to hero. Tarzan learns all about the "Strangers Like Me" while exploring his parents' tree house, which leads to deeper questions about his place in the world. The soldier Li Shang warns his hapless new recruits, "I'll Make a Man Out of You," in a delightfully ironic song as Mulan struggles to be all that she can be. The song is reprised with even more irony in act three, when the three soldiers helping Shang and Mulan need to dress in women's clothing in order for their plan to succeed.

## What Lies Beneath: The Art of the Subplot ⋯⋯⋯

One of the principle ways Disney storytellers create substantial screen stories from often uncinematic source material is the subplot. In most of these cases, the original story will cover only the main storyline, or A plot. The screenwriters still have the B and C plots to worry about—the subplots. While you may not be trying to turn a classic fairy tale into a ninety-minute screenplay, subplots are going to be every bit as important if you're hoping to craft a well-rounded and multidimensional story that will engage your audience over the course of a feature film.

The most effective and organic subplots have direct ties to the main plot, or at the least, offer reflections of the main characters, making the subplots integral parts of the overall story as opposed to awkward tangential paths that the audience is forced to go down. "You have to have something to cut to," is a familiar refrain that you'll hear from most Disney writers and directors, and it's as true for live-action screenwriters as it is for them, but you have to ensure that what you're cutting to has a compelling reason to be in your story.

Subplots generally focus on the secondary characters and frequently mirror the main character's situation. Lucifer, the cat in

*Cinderella*, is a direct reflection, terrorizing the household mice as Lady Tremaine and the wicked stepsisters make life miserable for Cinderella. And just as Hercules must prove himself a true hero in order to take his place among the gods, so too must his teacher Phil prove himself a trainer of heroes, worthy of placement among the constellations in the sky. Until their fateful meeting, Phil has been labeled a failure, but if he can successfully turn Hercules into a champion, both of their reputations will be assured.

Mushu may be acting as Mulan's guardian, but his own circumstances mirror those of his charge. Just as Mulan disgraces her family's honor by failing the matchmaker (setting her on fire is not the best way to impress her) and being too outspoken when her father is conscripted, Mushu has been demoted for conduct unbecoming a guardian. He must perform a deed that will honor his ancestors in order to reclaim his place in the firmament. Mulan and Mushu then travel a very similar path together: both disguise themselves (Mulan as a man, Mushu as a great dragon); both risk death if they are found out; both admit that their actions were selfishly motivated after their first efforts fail; and, finally, both are redeemed and restored to their original status at the film's conclusion.

One of the most effective subplots involves the Enchanted Objects in *Beauty and the Beast*. In early drafts, they were merely inanimate objects that had fallen under the same curse as the Beast. This was a minor story point that the fairy tale's audience was told, not shown, and didn't have much bearing on the story one way or the other. Turning these inanimate objects into multidimensional personalities, however, gave the audience additional characters to root for and sympathize with, and gave the filmmakers something to cut to.

Why do the Enchanted Objects work so well as the stars of their own subplot? Because they are inextricably linked to the same plot point that drives the main storyline. Cogsworth, Lumiere, Mrs. Potts, and Chip have just as great an interest in seeing the A plot resolved as does the Beast. They also provide continual reflections of their master, his prisoner, Belle, and the burgeoning relationship between the two of them. The audience learns something important about the main story and characters during every second the Enchanted Objects are onscreen. They are an integral and organic part of the story, not a random element that feels tacked on in order to pad the film's running time or provide extraneous comic relief. When *Beauty and the Beast* was reworked for its Broadway debut, and subsequently for the tenth-anniversary DVD release, the story team revived a musical sequence that had been cut from the film. The song encapsulates the central question of both the household staff and the Beast, their collective hope to be "Human Again." Its reintegration was seamless because the subplot of the Enchanted Objects is so interconnected with the main plot.

Subplots also focus on the main characters involved in secondary situations. The subplot of *Brother Bear* literally drives the main story forward at key points throughout the film. The A plot revolves around Kenai's new life as bear and the lesson he must learn about letting love guide his actions. That is what his relationship with the bear cub Koda is all about. Kenai doesn't realize it until the end of the film, but he is learning about love and the true meaning of brotherhood from Koda. The subplot revolves around Denahi's attempt to track and kill Kenai, and, by extension, Koda, which threatens that central relationship and everything Kenai must learn from it. It also places Kenai and Koda in nearly constant physical jeopardy, which gives the story a potent shot of adrenaline at key points throughout acts two and three.

In this case, the main plot and subplot are literally related by blood. Kenai and Denahi are brothers, and Kenai and Koda are becoming brothers. Kenai is learning from Koda, and Denahi is threatening not only that process but also their very lives. The ultimate connection between the main plot and subplot is Kenai and Denahi's need to learn the same thing: you must let love guide your actions. Kenai needs to learn it in order to become a man; Denahi needs to learn it in order to let both of his brothers go and to become a better man. Both characters are driven by the death or apparent death of a brother; and both eventually come to a place where they're guided by love and brotherhood and not by hatred and vengeance. The only real difference is that one character is making that journey as a bear, and the other is making it in human form.

Such intimate connections between a story's characters and plot points are hallmarks of a good subplot. First and foremost, your subplots must provide a vital link back to action of the main storyline and everything that is at stake in it. Wherever possible, they must also turn the spotlight on supporting characters, who should be interesting in and of themselves while illuminating new and compelling dimensions of the lead characters. If it can fulfill both of these roles, your subplot will provide you with more than enough strong story material to cut to, especially on the long and winding road that is act two.

Subplots that don't work can be found in abundance and are fairly easy to spot. The next time you're in a theater and suddenly feel as if you're watching a completely different movie, you'll know you're seeing a subplot that the filmmakers have failed to derive organically from their main story. By the same token, any time you find yourself thinking, Here comes the comic relief, you're likely enduring thinly drawn supporting characters that have little to say about the main characters. These cardboard cutouts likely can't carry their own B plot, much less contribute to the resolution of the A plot. You know them when you see them, so don't be part of the problem by writing them.

# Believability—The Art and Soul of Disney Characters ••••••••••••••••••••••••••••

*Sometimes we say the secret to Disney animation is 'story, story, story.' But the strength of any good story comes from 'character, character, character.' Create a compelling character and the audience will follow the story.*[42]

—Thomas Schumacher, former president,
Disney Feature Animation

What is the first thing you think of when you hear the name *Disney*? For many people, the answer to that question is, *characters*. Disney characters. The two words are almost synonymous at this point. From Mickey and Minnie to Kenai and Koda, The Walt Disney Studios has created a bigger stable and left a richer legacy of beloved characters than almost any other entertainment company in history. An emphasis on well-defined characters, whether princesses, animals, or cutlery, along with the mandate for a good story well told, has always been the cornerstone of Disney productions, from Walt's earliest short cartoons to the studio's latest animated features.

"Mickey's a nice fellow," said Walt, "who never does anybody any harm, who gets in scrapes through no fault of his own but always manages to come up grinning. . . . When people laugh at Mickey Mouse it's because he's so human; and that is the secret of his popularity." Like the best and most enduring of live-action movie characters, Mickey became a stand-in for the audience, enabling moviegoers everywhere to vicariously live, love, learn, and win through him. He became more than just their friend; he was one of them.

Walt had an unerring sense of what Mickey would and wouldn't do, and he firmly believed that moviegoers would come to have that same sense. And he was right. Mickey would always be Mickey, and the audience could count on that. Their particular enjoyment of the Disney cartoons came from seeing how this indefatigable personality would react to each new scenario. Before too long, Mickey couldn't do anything out of character because the audience wouldn't stand for it, and neither would Walt.

None of the supporting characters may have been the Everyman that Mickey was, but that didn't make it any harder for the audience to relate to them and they were soon to become superstars in their own right. Who among us hasn't felt the blissful ignorance (and innocence) of Goofy, the barely contained (and often not at all contained) frustration of Donald, the steadfast loyalty of Pluto, or even the gleeful, "Let's see what we can mess with next" mischievousness of Chip 'n' Dale? These characters all became mirrors, offering reflections of the different personalities among us, or, more often than not, the different parts of ourselves. That is why audiences immediately responded to them, and that is why they still endure today.

"I try to build a full personality for each of our cartoon characters," said Walt early on, "to make them personalities." The key word was *personality*. Walt knew that personality—the distinctive, visible characteristics of an individual—is the key to story, and, equally, that story can be the key to personality. The audience had to buy the personality in order to believe the story, and it was the story that enabled Walt and his storytellers to really bring out the individual personalities of their characters.

Until a character becomes a personality, it can't be believed, and you have to believe these animated stories. Without personality, the character may do funny or interesting things, but unless people are able to identify themselves with the character, its actions will seem unreal. And without personality, a story cannot ring true to an audience.

—Walt Disney

Put Goofy or Donald Duck in the exact same situation as Mickey, and you could expect completely different results. That was because, unlike many other cartoon stars of the period, the Disney characters were not interchangeable. Their individual personalities were much too strong, and story and character were too intricately connected to just change a character's name on the title card. The complex, symbiotic relationship between story and character at The Walt Disney Studios had begun.

The "selling" of characters and stories was going to take on a new and much greater importance when it came time to attempt a feature film. Suspension of disbelief while maintaining an audience's interest was one thing when the films were seven minutes long, but what about when they were seventy, or later eighty and ninety minutes long? The illusion of life was only going to become more critical.

The nine years between *Steamboat Willie* and *Snow White and the Seven Dwarfs*, which saw the production of dozens of Mickey Mouse short cartoons and the Silly Symphonies, taught Walt and his artists more than enough to get them started, enabling them to create characters believable enough to carry an eighty-three-minute feature and, more to the point, to tell the audience a story. In 1937 and happily ever after, The Walt Disney Studios had all the raw story materials they would need for everything that would follow: animated characters that were just as three-dimensional as flesh-and-blood actors; visually expressed action and motivation for those characters that were so well defined that the features would have worked just as well as silent films; and the ancient archetypes that would yield every class of Disney character to come: heroes, villains, love interests, parental figures, and comedic sidekicks. All thanks to the audience's unwavering belief in the illusion of life.

## To Tell the Truth:
## Belief = Sincerity Wrapped in Appeal ···········

Characters have two essential roles in any screenplay: to serve the story and to tell the truth. In order for them to do either one of these things effectively, the audience must believe in them. When an actor gives a flawless performance, the audience usually just accepts it without even thinking about it. They get caught up in the story and believe what they're seeing without stopping to consider the actor's "technique," or "approach to the craft," or any other *Inside the Actor's Studio* terms. However, when the audience sees a bad performance, it's just about all they can think about. It yanks them right out of the movie, destroying the art of storytelling in the process.

> *The first thing you have to have is a set of characters that can carry you through the story once they're established. That's the most important part. It's like a train leaving the station without the passengers. If you don't have characters from the word go, you don't have the story really started. I'm very familiar with the characters before I get into the story. If I know them well, I can develop the story.*[43]
>
> —Bill Peet, story artist

*It's sincerity packaged in appeal. Sincerity means you have to believe it.*[44]

—Glen Keane, animator

Screenwriters and story artists may be acting with a typewriter or pencil as opposed to their bodies and voices, but they are drawing on their own relationships, life experiences, and worldview just as surely as any actor or actress. Audiences have believed in Disney characters since the early days of Mickey Mouse, and this relationship between Disney and its audience has continued for over seventy-five years. The writers, directors, and animators responsible for bringing these characters to life have been doing something right, but what is it? What is the secret to creating this quality of believability, this illusion of life?

Believability is sincerity packaged in appeal. It's impossible to reduce the magic of Disney characters to a simple formula, but those two words, *sincerity* and *appeal*, have been handed down to each new generation since Walt and his artists began to master their craft. Sincerity entails telling the truth and creating plausible behavior, on the printed page as well as the drawing board. Appeal concerns overall character design, from personality—specifically likeability—to physical appearance. Disney storytellers package sincerity and appeal to help create the sometimes elusive quality of believability that enables their characters to tell—and sell—their stories.

## You Remind Me of Me ••••••••••••••••••••••••••

Sincerity is truth in storytelling. Even in enchanted realms of talking animals, dancing flatware, and flying pirate ships, writers have an obligation to tell the truth through their characters. And those characters have to ring true for the audience to accept them. Writers build characters trait by trait, flaw by flaw, behavior by behavior, instilling a great deal of themselves and people they know into their creations. That is the only way for viewers to see themselves in the personalities onscreen; the only way for them to truly identify with and relate to the characters and thus everything that's happening to them in the story.

When storytellers successfully make this magical connection, we as the audience feel as if we are the characters, and that is precisely because they were born of us to begin with. Ariel is considered a landmark character because she completely reinvented the concept of the traditional Disney princess. Instead of creating another passive beauty sitting around waiting for her prince to come and whisk her off to happily ever after (a perfectly acceptable notion in an earlier era), the story team made Ariel a thoroughly modern teenager, adolescent angst and all.

That truthful characterization continued throughout the animation process. Using the character in the script and on the storyboards as a starting point, Supervising Animator Glen Keane brought some of his own unique life experiences and relationships to Ariel. "As animators here at Disney, our biggest challenge is not only to make the characters move, but also to make them breathe," says Glen. "They have to appear to be thinking and making their own decisions. You have to see the thinking process. Whenever I do a scene where that comes across, then I feel like I've accomplished something."[45]

> A good test of whether you like somebody or not is to see them start to head off in a direction they shouldn't be going in, and if you're rooting for them not to, that means you love them, somehow. Something has clicked between you and that person.[46]
>
> —Glen Keane, animator

One of Glen's inspirations was a photograph of his wife, which he kept on his desk. He instilled in Ariel some of his wife's pluck, optimism, and, yes, even her stubbornness to create a character that ceased to be a series of drawings and became a living, breathing person (albeit one with a long, blue-green fish tail). Suddenly, this little mermaid was someone that everyone in the audience could relate to: mothers and fathers, sisters and brothers, and those thoroughly modern teenage girls themselves. That's because Ariel was created with sincerity and thus possessed the sincerity to tell the truth.

"Write as though your characters live in our world," advises Chris Sanders. "One of the things I enjoy about *Lilo & Stitch* is that, even though the characters are drawn as these very caricature creatures, you would never mistake Lilo for anything but a real person. She acts like a real person. I set up a world in which if Lilo fell down, she'd hurt herself, she wouldn't just bounce like Roger Rabbit. Those are the things I particularly like. If the character's indestructible it's going to be hard to empathize with that character."[47]

Not every character needs to be likable, obviously—villains certainly come to mind—but inherently unlikable and even unsympathetic characters can be strangely appealing in their own way. Audiences certainly have connected with Michael Corleone in *The Godfather* trilogy, they've even sympathized with the once noble war hero's fall from grace and morality and turned him into something of an anti-hero in the process. And that is because, on some level, they see aspects of themselves in him, as "bad" as he is, and thus relate to him whether they like him or not. That's an important point to remember: you don't necessarily have to like someone in order to relate to them.

> We have created characters and animated them in the dimension of depth, revealing through them to our perturbed world that the things we have in common far outweigh those that divide us.
> —Walt Disney

# When They're Bad, They're Better ••••••••••••••

Villains are among the most popular Disney characters, and have been from the very beginning. After all, they, too, possess some of the same personality traits and human foibles as their heroic counterparts, all of which come from their very human creators and the experiences and relationships they bring to the creative process.

Frank Thomas and Ollie Johnston, two more of Walt's Nine Old Men of animation know a thing or two about villains. "All of us are potential villains," they wrote in the appropriately named book *The Disney Villain*. "If we are pushed far enough, pressured beyond our breaking point, our self-preservation system takes over and we are capable of terrible villainy."[48] What separates the heroes from the villains, of course, are the choices they make to achieve their goal.

While every Disney villain may have a relatively questionable agenda, how they go about realizing their twisted dreams is a function of the art (or, in this case, the dark art) of characterization. Some are frightening, others upsetting, but all are interesting and often very funny at the same time. The extremes of their physical designs and personalities contribute to their humorous aspects, when they become desperate to achieve their goals, their behavior often grows so broad as to be absurd. "We all have funny little ways," said Walt, who didn't actually like to use the word *evil* to describe his heroes' opposition. A villain's desires are just as worthy as those of their opponent. "I'm not bad," says Jessica Rabbit, as would the Disney villains. "I'm just drawn that way."

There are many different shades of villainy, but the audience always needs to have a clear idea of the villain's motivations and tactics, or their contribution to your story's construction will be vastly diminished. In fact, a villain's desires often help create the spine of the story and drive the action. Cruella De Vil wants the Dalmatian puppies, setting the entire story into motion. Scar wants Mufasa's kingdom for himself, leading to a deadly palace coup and exile for the young prince Simba. At other times, the villain's intentions are a bit more intangible. The stepmother in *Cinderella*, motivated by jealousy, resentment, and greed, thinks of nothing but her own material wealth and comfort. To that end, she constantly plots to keep her beautiful stepdaughter out of sight so that her own daughters might have a better chance at marrying well.

The Queen of Hearts in *Alice in Wonderland* is a comparatively weak villain because there is no indication of why she behaves the way she does and no revelation of what she wants. A character who doesn't *want* anything isn't, technically speaking, even a character— it's a facade. The only insight into anyone's behavior in Wonderland is the Cheshire Cat's oversimplified summation, "We're all mad here." Although the Queen keeps barking, "Off with her head!," the audience has no understanding of her motivation and thus no way of relating to the character or connecting to the story. This, combined with Alice's infuriated reactions to the Queen and the other maniacal characters that relentlessly pop in and out of the film, eventually causes many viewers to lose interest. While visually stunning, *Alice* is a frustrating narrative. Ward Kimball, another of Walt Disney's Nine Old Men, summed up the *Alice* experience nicely when he called the film a "loudmouthed vaudeville show."[49]

Storytellers also need to strike an equal emotional balance between villains and heroes, or their "victims." After all, *someone* has to suffer the ill effects of the antagonist's machinations. "If there is no victim," said Frank and Ollie, "there is no villainy, only threatening potential."[50] If the audience is sympathetic to the victim, they will find the villain that much more threatening and position themselves squarely in the hero's corner. But, as the animators add, "It is a lopsided equation."[51] They note that the power to do evil is greater than the power to do good. The villain has a strategy and can prepare in advance. The hero, on the other hand, must think on his feet and needs to adhere to a strict moral code. The villain does not. Drama is heightened as we watch the hero struggle to avoid sinking to the villain's level and make choices against their character.

Once again, an old storytelling cliché rings true: your hero is only as strong as your villain. But don't confuse strength with numbers. Too many villains, like too many cooks in the kitchen, can spoil a potentially magical alchemy (or an entire film franchise—just look at Joel Schumacher's neon-and-molded-rubber-villain–laden film *Batman & Robin* if you require further proof). Speaking of Robins, in Disney's *Robin Hood*, the titular hero faces the neurotic Prince John, the bullying Sheriff of Nottingham, and the spineless Sir Hiss, but their agendas are too similar and don't possess enough nuance to justify their collective screen time. With villains, less is definitely more.

## Dis-Functional Families ........................

Stepmothers have gotten a decidedly bad rap over the years, largely due to the behavior of a single character, Lady Tremaine in Cinderella. They have fared a lot better in real life, thankfully, but in Disney films, stepmothers are villains, plain and simple. But Lady Tremaine is only one branch on Disney's dysfunctional family tree. So many parental "limbs" are missing so often in the animated features that it begs an obvious question: why do so many Disney heroes find themselves in these difficult family situations?

Fairy tales were crafted with the intention of guiding their readers through the dangerous and confusing events of everyday existence, with a moral lesson thrown in for good measure. Children have a lot to understand as they mature, and wondering why a parent may be sweetness and light one moment then turn into an angry "monster" the next is an important question that needs to be answered. In a child's mind, it is easier to separate the parent into two different figures. For example, the kind and loving provider is their real mother, while the cold and threatening disciplinarian is some sort of imposter—a "stepmother." Bruno Bettelheim, author of the influential *The Uses of Enchantment: The Meaning and Importance of Fairy Tales*, wrote, "The fantasy of the wicked stepmother not only preserves the good mother intact, it also prevents having to feel guilty about one's angry thoughts . . . about her. Thus, the fairy tale suggests how the child may manage the contradictory feelings, which would otherwise overwhelm him...."

Since a large number of Disney films are based on fairy tales, this aspect of the genre comes with the territory. Dealing with an evil parent, or even with the loss of a parent, places the main character of the story into an extremely dramatic situation from the start and it can only increase the dramatic tension from there. This is especially true when the stepparent in question is trying to prevent you from meeting your one true love, keeping you locked away in a secret tower, trying to feed you a poisoned apple, or any number of comparable domestic situations.

Another side of this phenomenon addresses the simple issue of maturation. "We have many Disney characters who don't have parents," acknowledges Don Hahn. "And you must realize that the lack of a parent or the loss of a parent is a signal flag for the onset of growth. Tarzan discovers a photo of his parents in a tree house; Mufasa is killed, leaving Simba alone and full of guilt; Mowgli is orphaned and searches for himself using Baloo and Bagheera as his parents, until he meets the little girl. It's funny how many times the idea of loss of parents always ends up with finding a spouse. It just supports that idea of growth, growing up, maturing. Aladdin is the orphan who finds Jasmine; Cinderella is the stepdaughter who finds the prince; the Beast and Belle both lack at least one parent and find each other; and Tramp, the loner, finds Lady. There are many exceptions, but the macro theme of finding love and acceptance no matter who you are is very common in our films."[52]

# Characters You Can Warm Up To ●●●●●●●●●●●●●●●●●

One of the words most often used to describe favorite Disney characters is *warmth*. When an animated feature doesn't work, nine times out of ten critics will talk about how it lacked warmth, or how the audience just didn't warm up to the characters. Warmth derives from appeal, especially when that appeal is wrapped around sincerity.

*Snow White* and *Cinderella* were more artistically and commercially successful than *Alice in Wonderland* and *Sleeping Beauty* because they both feature much warmer and more appealing leading ladies. You could argue that this is because Walt Disney himself was much more personally involved with those first two films than the other two, but the fact remains that Snow White and Cinderella are just warmer, more appealing, and more human characters than Princess Aurora and Alice, period.

Aurora, the sleeping beauty of the film's title, isn't very well developed as a main character, much less as a victim. She never meets her adversary Maleficent, as she is isolated—and ostensibly protected—from all harm from the moment of her birth. "Even when she climbed the stairs to the spinning wheel at the castle, she was hypnotized and unaware of what was happening," wrote animators Ollie Johnston and Frank Thomas. "A few of us wondered if she would have been a more interesting character if she had come face-to-face with Maleficent and had somehow been forced against her will to prick her finger and die."[53] Because of the lack of obstacles in Aurora's way, it is Prince Phillip, fighting the dragon into which Maleficent transforms herself, and saving the castle's inhabitants, whom we can relate to and sympathize with as the real "victim" in the story.

When the main character is constantly frustrated—not physically, but in their reactions—so, too, is the audience. "Most of the characters Alice met in Wonderland were rude or dangerous," said Frank and Ollie, "and all of them caused her some kind of trouble. But her reaction to them was annoyance and exasperation rather than the fear we expected from the victims of our villains."[54] Alice's constant irritation and resulting bad mood don't exactly endear her to the audience, eroding their one connection to everything that is going on in the story.

Sincerity and appeal, wrapped snugly around each other and working together, create the quality of believability that the most effective Disney characters possess. It is that quality that enables storytellers to share universal truths through those characters. The audience may not be able to articulate why they see such truth in the Disney characters, but they believe it when they see it.

## Action is Character ····································

A character is as a character does. That may sound like something Forrest Gump might have said, but it is actually a pretty accurate summation of good character development. What characters *do* defines and reveals who they *are*. As we must sometimes learn the hard way in life, what someone says and what someone does are often two completely different things. A person (or an animal, or an alien, or even a willow tree) can say anything, but what they choose to do tells us so much more about them. It's something tangible; we can see it; it is. We should never have to take a character's word when it comes to who they are; let us see them in action so we can come to our own conclusions. Action truly is character, another corollary of the classic "Show, don't tell" rule of screenwriting.

> *The important thing to us is what the characters are doing, not so much what they're saying.*[55]
>
> —Winston Hibler, story artist

"Let's imagine a beautiful woman pulling up at the Oscars," says Broose Johnson, head of story, *Brother Bear*. "She gets out of her limousine, spits, and starts walking. You would say, 'What was that all about?' This gorgeous woman just spat on the sidewalk and doesn't seem to feel too bad about it. Right away, you're interested. What's her story? Why did she choose to spit at the Oscars, and in such a way as not to hide it? Was she spitting because she had something in her teeth? Does she hate the Oscars? She just made a choice to do something, and all of a sudden, she's an interesting character because she made an interesting choice, and this simple choice defines her. Her next choice will define her further. So, the challenge in creating a great character is in finding great situations in which he or she can make the kind of choices that will reveal the character we need to build, all the while keeping in mind that it needs to underline the overall theme we're wanting to project."[56]

Chris Sanders agrees. "Why did that character do that? Why? You'd be surprised how many people want characters to behave in a completely logical manner. There doesn't need to be a solid motivation or complex explanation for everything a character does. You do a hundred things that are completely illogical all day long. As you're driving to work, you decide to stop and buy *Road and Track* magazine because you want to look at a race car. Why? Do you own a race car? No, but you look at them because you like them. With characters you have to set into them likes, dislikes, weaknesses, strengths; and I love little illogical things like that that begin to make a character. I think a character's accessibility is through their imperfections, and not through their virtues, necessarily."[57]

There is the temptation, especially in the world of animation, to get too hung up on what a character looks like. Sometimes the nature of a character calls for the outside to reflect what's on the inside, as with the Witch in *Snow White and the Seven Dwarfs*. Her appearance is only the result of a magic spell—the character is every bit as evil in her original form as the deceivingly beautiful Queen. In designing the character of Quasimodo in *The Hunchback of Notre Dame*, James Baxter put a stress on horizontal shapes instead of vertical ones so that "his shape contrasts deliberately with the other major characters, especially Frollo, who is very tall and Gothic. Frollo seems to fit in with the Gothic architecture while Quasi doesn't." Baxter also had to deal with an unusual appearance of a character who still needed to be agile and energetic. "He's deformed but not disabled," says Baxter. "His being bent over was a metaphor for his wanting to hide. We wanted him to wrap in on himself, able to bend over and cower in his most oppressed moments."[58] But who is the man, the audience asks when watching Quasi and Frollo. And who is really the monster?

And what about the Beast? He may have an outwardly horrific appearance, but there is a good heart beating deep within, as evidenced by his choice to release Belle so she can go to the rescue of her father toward the end of act two. Looks can and often should be deceiving. A character's choices and their resulting actions should define who they are on the inside, where it counts.

Looks aren't all that important to begin with. Leave your character's appearance to the animator, or the casting department, or the costume designer unless it's a significant story point, such as Quasimodo's deformity. Clothes don't make the man or the mouse. Before you write multiple paragraphs exhaustively describing their physical appearance, from the color of their hair to the cut of their clothes, present your characters with an interesting choice instead. Or put them in an environment or situation in which their true nature is revealed, for good or for ill. Nobody wants to see Mulan running a neighborhood diner, or Baloo and Mowgli storming the beach at Normandy. Put your characters in situations that will enable them to be who they are meant to be.

"Character and story are so intermingled that it's impossible to separate them," says Broose Johnson. "If you have James Bond in *Sleepless in Seattle*, he'd no longer be James Bond. A character is defined by the choices he makes, so if you never give him James Bondish choices to make, he'll never show you that he's James Bond. You'd probably never know Mr. Bond could save the world if you had him working in a flower shop."[59]

And don't put all your money where your character's mouth is. Rather than give them an entire speech in which they share their own inevitably skewed self-image with anyone onscreen who will listen, have them instead take a defining action when nobody is watching except the audience. Then *we* can decide who they really are and what it is they want, and why. In the musical number "One Jump Ahead" we first meet our brash young hero Aladdin stealing bread as he evades the vizier Jafar's goons. At this first glance, he appears to be out for himself; his actions indicating a selfish, arrogant punk. But then, as he sits down to eat with his monkey Abu, two smaller street urchins approach, even more desperate for a meal than the "street rat." Aladdin willingly gives up his food to them and the audience sees what kind of guy he really is, by this simple, wordless act of kindness. (Abu's egocentric personality never deviates from our first impression.) So it comes as no surprise later when Aladdin grants the Genie his freedom at the end. It has already been established that Aladdin really is a diamond in the rough.

"I happen to think personality, character, and story go hand in hand," says Peter Schneider, former president of The Walt Disney Studios. "I happen to think story is your control, from which characters and personality must work as your framework to allow the entertainment, the jokes, the fun to happen. My concern with personality is indulgence. One has to be very careful not to become indulgent with a personality and characters, to the exclusion of everything else."[60]

Another strong example of actions speaking much louder than words can be seen in *Beauty and the Beast*, when Belle willingly takes her father's place, presumably forever, as a prisoner in the Beast's castle. The audience has already seen Belle's yearning for adventure beyond her provincial town and knows what a sacrifice she is making by imposing upon herself a life sentence within the dark, dank confines of a remote castle. It is the single worst fate that could possibly befall her, and yet she willingly embraces it out of love for her father. And it speaks volumes. In this way a complex, engaging character is built, choice by choice, action by action, consequence by consequence. Talk is cheap, but action is character.

## "I Want It, I Want It, I Want It!" or "What's My Motivation?"

A character is only as strong as the goal they are trying to achieve and whatever is preventing them from achieving it. In the simplest terms, what do they want? Or, as actors often say, what is their motivation? The answer should be as simple as it is powerful. The strongest characters have a clear, concise objective, and realizing that objective is the single most important thing in the world to them. It has to be to sustain a feature film. But it never comes easy. What fun would that be? To the contrary, characters must endure a vast array of opposing forces, all massing to prevent them from getting what they want. Strong opposition is the only way for characters to truly prove their worth and earn the audience's confidence, respect, and sympathy—to make the audience root for them. Regardless of whether it's as vast as the undead army in *The Black Cauldron* or as seemingly minute as the threat of the falling rose petals in *Beauty and the Beast*.

Most of the strongest Disney heroes and heroines want something very simple, very personal, and very important. Pinocchio wants to be a real boy. Ariel is desperate to be part of the human world. Jim Hawkins wants to prove his worth. They all desperately want something, and over the course of ninety minutes or so, the audience desperately wants them to have it. And that something has to be very important to the protagonist if it's going to be of any importance to the audience.

In most Disney animated features, there is one defining moment in which the audience learns what that special something is for the main character. In that moment, they essentially see an encapsulation of the entire character and learn what it is they want most out of life. In Disney animated features, this defining moment often takes the form of a song. In *The Little Mermaid*, Ariel sings "Part of Your World," an ode to Prince Eric and life on land. Belle proclaims her desire for adventure beyond her small village's borders at the end of her song, "Belle," early in act one of *Beauty and the Beast*. And Simba recruits hundreds of jungle animals to build an elaborate production number on his longing for a regal future in *The Lion King*'s "I Just Can't Wait to Be King." The audience knows what those characters want in no uncertain terms, and, more to the point, wants them to have it.

If the consequences of not getting what they want aren't high enough, the audience isn't going to take much interest in the story or care whether the character achieves their goal or not. This is the protagonist's central motivation, which should be as important to the character as the air they breathe. It poses some very tough questions for the character; questions that any audience is going to want to see answered. What is it worth to you? What are you willing to sacrifice to get it? At what price do dreams come true? And what price are you willing to pay? Over the past one hundred years of American film, audiences have told filmmakers that they believe in truth and justice, true love, personal identity, a happy life, and, in the simplest of

> On every movie, when you start off, there's so much time spent sitting back and thinking how to do a character. But, finally, you've got to plunge in, start drawing, and inevitably, your first attempts are terrible. Terrible. You have to go through that bad stage because, later, it's worth it.[61]
> —Mike Show, animator, *Hercules*

cases, the worthiness of survival, of life itself. These are all worth playing a high-stakes game for. And that is why we see so many characters pursuing those very things, from Dorothy Gale to Rick Blaine to Atticus Finch to Luke Skywalker.

Another question to be asked and answered is what the character must sacrifice in order to realize their dreams. Tarzan must give up life with the gorillas and his beloved mother Kala to be part of Jane's "civilized" society. Simba leaves behind a carefree life of *hakuna matata*, free from all responsibility (and wouldn't we all like to live that way?), to eventually face his father's killer and the judgment of the other lions in his pride to meet his destiny as king of the jungle. Hercules would willingly sacrifice his own life if it would bring Megara back from the dead. The more your characters are willing to sacrifice, the more important we know their dreams to be, and the more the audience will get behind them and want to see those dreams come true.

## Can't We All Just Get Along? No! What Fun Would That Be? ....................

Strong motivation makes for a powerful character, one that is driven by desire and desperate to overcome anyone or anything that stands in their way. It's the stuff drama is made of, to paraphrase Sam Spade in *The Maltese Falcon*. Strong opposition makes for an even stronger story. In order to create that strong opposition, naturally you need strong characters, specifically the main protagonist and antagonist— your hero and villain. They are the central characters that drive the story, and their relationship is a deeply symbiotic one, as evidenced by yet another old screenwriting maxim: "A hero is only as good as the villain who opposes him." The question for you is who or what opposes your hero? The answer will determine just what kind of conflict drives your story; and out of conflict comes all drama.

The most common kind of conflict pits one character or group of characters against another, that classic freshman English writing-class concept known as "man versus man." In Disney's animated features, this struggle may take the form of princess versus evil queen, mermaid versus sea witch, lion versus lion, or boy versus cyborg, but the principle is the same. This kind of conflict sets the stage for the traditional hero versus villain scenario that has created the drama in so many of our most enduring stories, in print, on stage, and on screen. These conflicts appeal to the audience precisely because they are so intensely personal.

Think of Snow White and the Queen, Peter Pan and Captain Hook, or Cruella De Vil and those 101 Dalmatians. Life itself is at stake in their conflicts: death is the consequence of failure to achieve their goals. The conflict between these characters is clear, immediate, and unique to the parties involved. Nothing humanizes the epic struggle between good and evil so well as the strong personalities of our beloved heroes and the villains we love to hate. Storytellers make it a lot easier for an audience to sympathize with and root for their hero when the opposition is so sharply focused on one vile, hateful, scheming face.

This is just as true in live-action, too, where the ongoing battle between good guys in white hats and bad guys in black hats has fueled more than a century of American film. John Wayne spent an entire career fighting against the forces of tyranny in the dusty streets of the old West and on battlefields all over the world. Luke Skywalker engaged in a sprawling, three-film struggle against his father, the dark lord Darth Vader. Batman has faced his Rogue's Gallery of infamous archvillains in no fewer than five mediums. And James Bond has saved the world from upward of twenty evil geniuses at this point. There's nothing like a good fight to bring an audience together.

A second form of conflict finds a character squaring off against the natural world. This is humankind versus nature, or, in the case of *Bambi*, nature versus humankind. Once again, anything from animals to dinosaurs to robots can stand in for people, as long as nature remains the opposing force. Humankind versus nature may be the story's central conflict, as in *Brother Bear*, or a secondary level of opposition, as can be seen in *Pinocchio*, *Pocahontas*, and *Tarzan*.

Sometimes the humankind versus nature conflict is even more complex than it first appears. In *Brother Bear*, Kenai's central conflict is with the natural world, and yet he spends most of the film as part of that world, in the form of the very creature he most despises, no less. This complication enables the audience to see both sides of the conflict with equal clarity, and they often find themselves rooting for different characters for different reasons throughout the story.

The main protagonists in *Pocahontas* and *Tarzan* may be human beings, but they are fighting against their own "kind" on behalf of the natural world, giving nature a human face. In those instances, the central conflict still involves character versus character (Native Americans against Colonists, Tarzan against Clayton). Humanity versus nature operates on an intricate, secondary level, bringing an intriguing level of complexity to the overall conflict.

Humanity versus nature has long been a favorite theme among storytellers in all mediums. It is a common element of the animated features, and it has also served as the basis for some of the most memorable live-action films in movie history. These stories include adaptations of classic books and entirely original stories, from *Moby Dick* and *Jaws* to *Twister* and *Armageddon*. In the 1970s, the conflict took the form of an entire series of natural-disaster movies, including *The Poseidon Adventure*, *The Towering Inferno* (well, nature had a little help from humanity in that one), and *Earthquake*. The natural world can be a big, scary place, and every once in a while it's going to want to show us who's boss.

As the level of conflict grows ever larger, spreads outward, and becomes even more encompassing, we enter the realm of humanity versus society. This form of conflict pits an individual or group against an element of the overall social structure, be it their community, school, church, or government—to name just a few of the more common antagonists. Since most people (and our animal, alien, and marine stand-ins) possess an often desperate need for love and acceptance, such a conflict presents the protagonist with some seriously raised stakes. As anyone who has ever experienced high school can tell you, nobody wants to feel like a misfit or an outcast, and will do just about anything to avoid or get out of such a situation.

Although a Disney animated feature is not the ideal venue for biting social commentary, the character versus society conflict is a surprisingly common element in some of the studio's more complex stories, as in *Pocahontas* and *Tarzan*. Any character who is made to feel different, and inferior because of their differences, or who is ostracized in any way, is unwillingly engaged in this type of conflict with the world around them.

Sometimes the societal conflict is a relatively minor component of the story, and is not the end of the world for the protagonist. This is the case with Belle in *Beauty and the Beast*, who is merely looked upon as a bit eccentric because of her love of books and unwillingness to marry the most popular guy in town, the insufferable Gaston.

In *Dumbo*, however, the subject of society's scorn and ridicule is a child, unable to stand up for himself. When Dumbo's mother attempts to defend him from the narrow-mindedness and ridicule of his tormentors, she is labeled a "mad elephant" and physically segregated from their circus community. In this story even the defender of a misfit is forsaken, resulting in a baby's horrific separation from his mother. And in *The Hunchback of Notre Dame*, such a conflict destroys the self-esteem and even threatens the very life of poor Quasimodo. He endures a lonely existence, sequestered in a remote bell tower, because the vile Frollo has convinced him that society could never accept such a hideous creature. And so Quasimodo wiles away his days, dreaming of just one day "Out There."

In live-action films, humanity versus society conflicts often take the form of serious social drama. Such stories are often an attempt to call attention to the world's collective ills and occasionally propose solutions to right some of society's wrongs. Societal conflict lies at the heart of some of the greatest film dramas of the past half-century, including *To Kill a Mockingbird*, *Network*, *Norma Rae*, and *Silkwood*. Whether it is the central conflict of your story or an added level of complication for your protagonist, a humanity versus society theme will always be a compelling subject for exploration. Conflict between the individual and society has been an inevitable part of the human condition since we first began to live in groups.

Sometimes conflict heads in the exact opposite direction and turns inward, creating the most personal and bitter kind of struggle, a man versus himself scenario. There is a reason that the cliché, "You are your own worst enemy," has become so familiar—it's true. Nobody knows how to hurt, torture, and ultimately destroy us better than we do ourselves. That's because we know where our own weak spots are, what will cut us right to the quick, and when to strike. To make matters worse, such conflicts often rage right alongside problems we may be having with any of the outside forces we've examined thus far. In other words, conflict within the psyche is a perfect device for pushing an already overburdened character right over the edge.

Most characters in the animated features don't experience exclusively internal conflicts, but they are often forced to grapple with inner demons while they're in the middle of some sort of external strife. Pinocchio may have his little wooden hands full with Honest John and Gideon, Stromboli, and Monstro the whale, but what is foremost on his mind the entire time? Becoming a real boy. He is consumed with "walking the straight and narrow path" so the Blue Fairy will transform him into a flesh-and-blood child for his father, Geppetto. Throughout the film, it is his own perceived personal failings that torture him more than anything the story's villainous characters could throw at him.

When Pinocchio realizes that Geppetto has been lost at sea as a result of his own selfishness and poor judgment, he finally begins to overcome petty temptations and frivolous indulgences and exhibits the qualities that will make him a real boy. He rescues his father from the belly of Monstro the whale, giving his own life in the process. The Blue Fairy rewards Pinocchio from his bravery and nobility by making him a real boy, knowing that his inner conflict has been resolved at last.

Another film in which the hero struggles with inner conflict is *Tarzan*. "Whenever we were confronted with a situation that didn't ring true, we talked a lot about how it related to things that went on in our lives," says Kevin Lima, *Tarzan*'s director. "We would always try to find ways to make the moments real. That's very important to me, to hook into something that's specific to real life. I think ultimately Tarzan is his own villain. He causes the downfall of his family himself. He gets pushed a bit by Clayton, but ultimately he acts on his own. It's not the classic Hero's Journey where there's a strong external force that is playing against him. Tarzan's conflict is internal, and we searched throughout the film to find ways to take his internal journey and make it external."[62]

The film's original climax, in which Tarzan battled Clayton aboard a burning ship, "worked wonderfully on its own," says Greg Perler, editor of *Tarzan*. "But when the sequence was edited together, we realized that we had somehow 'lost' the character of Tarzan in all the action." The conflict and confusion that the boy raised by gorillas had been experiencing and now needed to resolve was better exemplified in the tangled vine fight—an idea of Bob Tzudiker and Noni White's. "We were reluctant at first, but by shifting the action to the trees, the audience was placed in Tarzan's world. Throughout the scene, Clayton becomes more and more like the animals he's hunted."[63] The internal is made external.

Aladdin's entire hero's journey centers around his inability—his refusal—to be himself. He is so consumed by the fact that people judge him by his outward appearances and by what he has (or doesn't have), that he can't always allow himself to see his own inner worth and let it shine forth. If he did, others might see it, too, and judge him on his true merits instead. Once he gets hold of the lamp, it's his insistence on pretending to be something he's not that perpetuates this inner conflict until act three. He finally resolves the crisis within him when he realizes that it is his own inner goodness, strength, and innate worth that will enable him to triumph in his external conflicts with Jafar, Jasmine, and those judgmental subjects of Agrabah themselves.

The most complex stories feature a variety of conflicts that operate on different levels. Tales of misfit heroes such as Aladdin and Quasimodo feature protagonists who are either unhappy with themselves or can't find their place in the world. They are engaged in at least three different struggles at the same time. There is a raging internal conflict born of their chronic dissatisfaction with their lot in life and a desperate yearning for something more. On top of that there is an ongoing misunderstanding with the community around them, which would just as soon see these misfits disappear entirely, never to darken their doorstep again. And rounding out our hero's problems is a personal conflict with one powerful member of that society in particular, such as an evil vizier or a high-ranking member of the clergy. All three conflicts are intricately connected, as are their resolutions, and our heroes aren't likely to come to terms with any of their enemies until they've made peace with themselves. And you thought they were just cartoons!

## What's in a Theme? ............................

*If I can't find a theme, I can't make a film anyone else will feel. I can't laugh at intellectual humor. I'm just corny enough to like to have a story hit me over the heart.*

—Walt Disney

As we have seen, story and character are the twin engines that power the animated features, but if you were to expand the secret of their success by one essential ingredient, then *theme* would join that dynamic duo to form something of a "holy trinity" of story elements. What happens in a narrative and to whom is one thing, but what does the story *mean*? What meaning are the characters meant to take away from what they have experienced, and what are we as an audience meant to take away from the story we have just experienced? A story's theme is the message the storyteller hopes to send to the world—it's what they're trying to *say*.

Not all films have a strong theme, nor should they. I don't think anyone's looking for deep meaning in any one of the *Police Academy* films. And that's okay. There's nothing necessarily wrong with story for story's sake; or characters that entertain us for a couple of hours and then vanish from our hearts and minds forever. But theme is one of the keys to the creation of stories that endure forever, and characters that take up permanent residence in the lives of filmgoers around the world.

Theme has been an integral part of Disney animation from the very beginning, when "True love can conquer all" and "Always let your conscience be your guide" brought an added weight and substance to what had long been considered a children's medium. Theme became such a compelling means for Walt to enrich his narratives and reveal different dimensions of his characters during those first twenty years that when he began to share his stories and characters in three dimensions at Disneyland, the result was referred to as the world's first *theme* park.

Strong themes played an even more important role throughout the second golden age of animation, beginning with "Children should be free to live their own lives" in *The Little Mermaid*. This timely *and* timeless enduringly relevant story about an overprotective parent letting go and allowing his daughter to grow up and make her own choices was closely followed by the equally enduring "Don't judge a book by its cover" message of *Beauty and the Beast*. Much like Walt's before them, these new classics presented universal truths in engaging and accessible new ways, reaching and touching a thoroughly modern and increasingly cynical audience.

The themes emerging from the animated features became even more complex and sophisticated throughout the 1990s, continuing with the studio's follow-up to its first Best Picture nominee. At first glance, *Aladdin* appears to feature a "Don't judge a book by its cover" theme similar to that in *Beauty and the Beast*, which is evident in the Genie's frustrated "It's not what's on the outside but what's on the inside that counts" entreaties. But a closer look reveals an even deeper meaning.

"Freedom is the biggest theme," says co-director John Musker. "Everybody in the film is trapped by one thing or another. Aladdin is trapped by his social situation. The Genie is trapped in the lamp. Jafar feels trapped because he's got to answer to the Sultan, who he thinks is an idiot. The Sultan is trapped by a stupid law into trying to marry his daughter to someone she doesn't want to marry, and his daughter is trapped by the same law."[64]

*Aladdin*'s central theme revolving around the real and perceived obstacles that can keep us from personal freedom if we let them shows that we can only be truly free when we accept who we are and, in the process, escape from the individual traps we set for ourselves. "The biggest thing that we started with was the idea that it's not what you have on the outside," says co-director of *Aladdin* Ron Clements, "but what you are on the inside, that's important. Inner values opposed to superficial values. And that's the thread that runs through the movie. Aladdin gets the lamp and gets, presumably, this thing that's the answer to his problem. But this traps him even more, because he gets trapped into this role playing of being a prince, which he really is not.

And at the end of the movie, everybody is freed from his own trap to some degree—except Jafar."[65]

This theme of acceptance and freedom is illustrated through each of the main characters in some way and figures prominently in the specific roles they play in the plots and subplots that make up the overall story. A strong theme brings added weight and meaning to the story itself, and is revealed to the audience by most if not all of the major characters. In those instances, these three creative elements—story, character, and theme—are inextricably linked and virtually inseparable from one another.

*What theme allows you to do is create a clothesline to hang ideas on. If it doesn't fit on that clothesline, then it shouldn't be on there. What allows you to make that decision is asking which idea better illustrates the theme.[66]*

—Chuck Williams, producer, *Brother Bear*

It should be abundantly clear by now that there is no one right way to do things when it comes to crafting your screenplay, and that guiding principle extends to the evolution of theme. Having said that, however, it should be pointed out that, more often than not, theme emerges *from* a story and reveals itself *after* the fact. It rarely drives the initial spark of an idea because it is through the writing process that the writer himself discovers just what it is he's trying to say with this story and through these characters. In fact, after completing a long succession of rewrites, screenwriters often look at their final draft and exclaim, "Ah, so *that's* what I meant!"

Stories that begin with theme run the biggest risk of coming off as pedantic and preachy rather than objectively presenting life's universal truths in a way that is both accessible and relevant to the audience. In other words, it's much more important for you to say, "I want to tell a good story," or "I want to introduce people to these quirky characters," than "I want to tell the world that it's wrong to judge a book by its cover." More often than not, a writer who puts the cart before the horse and tries to impose a message on a story or characters that may not want or need it is going to find himself in trouble.

"You can have a theme," says producer Don Hahn, "but don't let the story serve the theme so much so that you don't have a good time telling the story. Then you feel like you're eating your broccoli or sitting at church hearing a boring sermon. And that's not fun. You should feel free enough to tell a story so that nobody leaves the movies saying, 'Ah, honey wasn't the theme of that movie, 'Don't judge a book by its cover,' great?' You know it intellectually, feel it, you understand that it unites the movie, but you're more likely to say, 'I felt so satisfied when he earned his place back at the end of the movie,' or 'I felt so satisfied that he reunited with his father.' It's got to be what's right for that story.

"Theme is a funny thing," adds Don. "Sometimes it is established very early, as in *Beauty and the Beast* and the 'Don't judge a book by its cover' theme. Other times it grows from the material or is 'reverse engineered' after you see the film a few times."[67]

That being said, the creators of *Beauty and the Beast* knew that their adaptation of the tale as old as time would retain the "Don't judge a book by its cover" message of the original story—the trick was to deliver that message in a compelling story with strong, three-dimensional characters in so doing. Likewise, the *Brother Bear* team had higher hopes for their story than the delivery of an "It's wrong to kill bears" message. They knew early on that they had something important to say about love and brotherhood, and massaged those themes into their final, complex message: "You can't truly become a man until you learn to make decisions based on love." But these instances are the exceptions and not the rule. In most cases, theme remains hidden deep within the fabric of your story and characters and slowly emerges throughout the writing process, gaining strength and clarity every step of the way.

"I think that there are other more generalist or 'macro' themes in Disney movies," says Don, "the greatest of which is the theme of the outcast being accepted, or his or her journey towards acceptance or growth. I think it is a theme that we all relate to and is in all the films.

"Maybe Joseph Campbell was the one who talked about life as 'a constant state of becoming.' Looking for the next higher self, sometimes reluctantly, is a very universal Disney theme. Pinocchio asks, 'When will I be a real boy?' Ariel wants to experience life with two legs instead of a tailfin. Aladdin, Hercules, and the Beast want to have people look beyond their street urchin, superhero, and ugly exteriors, respectively, and be seen for their real selves. This state of becoming is almost like peeling back the layers of an onion to reveal what's inside. We did this literally in *Atlantis*, where characters revealed more about themselves the further they traveled into the core of the earth. It was done more simply in *The Emperor's New Groove*, in which Kuzco learns about the profound meaning of love and life from the peasant, Pacha."[68]

You don't have to wait until your final draft to address the theme of your story. Chances are very good you will have begun to identify it long before then, and the refinement of that theme or themes becomes one of the primary objectives of the rewrite process. You can enhance your theme in each subsequent draft until it takes its rightful place alongside story and character as a major component of your screenplay. The trick is to arrive there organically and honestly—let your story and characters tell you what they mean. If both of those things begin to take on lives of their own—as they always do in a magical alchemy—you will indeed find that there is a deeper meaning and your script will reveal it to you, but only when it, and you, are ready. In fact, in some cases, an emerging theme can actually show you what's wrong with your story and give you an idea of how to fix or strengthen it. Such was the case with the most successful traditionally animated feature of all time.

## Long Live the King ............................

In the case of *The Lion King*, an emerging theme actually helped shape and focus the narrative as the story made its way through a lengthy development process. The project had been kicking around the studio since 1989, when the Feature Animation team expressed an interest to make another allegorical tale with an all-animal cast in the tradition of *Bambi*. They eventually landed on an African setting with lions in the leading roles. "When I came on board the project was described to me as *Bambi* in Africa with a little Hamlet thrown it—it was *Bamblet*,"[69] co-writer Irene Mecchi remembers.

*The Lion King* began its journey under the title *King of the Jungle* with co-directors Roger Allers and Rob Minkoff and *Beauty and the Beast* producer Don Hahn at the helm. They were determined to craft an ambitious coming-of-age story with a mythic structure, combining time-tested Shakespearean elements with the epic quality of grand religious tales. "*The Lion King* has a little bit of Moses, a little bit of Joseph—the prince being exiled from the tribe," says Don Hahn. "Also Hamlet—searching for the murderer of his father and being haunted by his father's ghost. The hero has to conquer many things, get over many obstacles, and return triumphant to his kingdom."[70]

But that would prove to be easier said than done. The production team spent the next three years or so flirting with a number of different titles and creative treatments and scripts, but no one clear storyline emerged from the process.

The production finally moved forward in earnest as the studio was putting the finishing touches on *Aladdin*, when most of the studio's animation talent was looking to sign on to their next project. *King of the Jungle* was widely considered to be something of a secondary effort; the prestige project that everyone wanted to join was *Pocahontas*. "It was the B picture," remembers head of story Brenda Chapman. "It was the one the A players weren't working on."[71] That gave *King* an underdog quality, instilling in its production crew an intense desire to rise above such humble beginnings and second-class status and prove their project's worth. With that lofty goal in mind, *King*'s creative leads set about assembling a story team that would enable them to do just that.

"Early on in the process we recruited Rob Minkoff and Roger Allers to direct,"[72] Don recalls. Allers, Minkoff, and Hahn put together what they termed a "brain trust" to solidify the story once and for all. In addition to Allers, Minkoff, and Hahn, the team consisted of head of story Brenda Chapman, production designer Chris Sanders, artistic coordinator Randy Fullmer, and *Beauty and the Beast* co-directors Gary Trousdale and Kirk Wise. Armed only with pushpins and drawing paper, the team spent two days hashing out the story, and walked away with a solid outline for the film. Screenwriters Irene Mecchi and Jonathan Roberts came aboard shortly thereafter and worked closely with Chapman's story team to continue to evolve the narrative.

"We had two days where we sat in my office," says Don, "Rob Minkoff and Roger Allers, Brenda Chapman, Kirk Wise, Gary Trousdale, Randy Fullmer, Chris Sanders, and myself and a bunch of legal pads and stuff, and if you look at those

> Let's face it, this lion cub gets framed for murder, we've got a wildebeest stampede, there's a singing warthog. Will it mean anything?[73]
>
> —Don Hahn, producer, *The Lion King*

and what the story was and you look at the movie two years later, the story didn't change structurally that much. It was still a story about a young, eager lion cub who was born into royalty and thought it would be an easy path. He was betrayed by his uncle, framed for the murder of his dad, and had to run away and learn to grow up with these 'lost boys' characters out in the woods. When he came back, he could defeat his uncle and claim his rightful place. It was about hard-earned lessons, which came out in those couple of days."[74]

The story and screenwriting teams embraced their emerging tale's *Hamlet* influence and turned their villain, Scar—until then a rogue lion with no blood relation to the pride—into Mufasa's brother and Simba's uncle, making his plot to overthrow the king a family affair and bringing an even deeper resonance to the central conflict. They also weren't shy about making a number of biblical allusions to the story of Joseph, about a young prince born into royalty and unjustly exiled, only to triumphantly return at a time of crisis to claim his rightful place as ruler. These and other narrative elements helped contribute to the film's overall mythic structure and epic scale, giving it the weight and gravity its creators had sought from the very beginning. Now all the story team needed was a guiding theme compelling enough to meet their ever-rising hopes and expectations.

"In a Disney animated feature, characters are vital, and so is a strong theme," says Don. "In fact, those two things are inseparable because the main characters—both the heroes and the villains—are expressions of the theme. *Aladdin* is about learning to be yourself. *Beauty and the Beast* reminds us not to judge a book by its cover. The problem with early drafts of *The Lion King* was that they lacked a clear theme. Finally we realized that the theme was responsibility. It's about leaving childhood and facing up to the realities of the world. In her early scripts, Linda Woolverton had begun to establish a structure that would allow this theme to be expressed. But that still left a lot of work to be done."[75]

*The Lion King* was, at its heart, a coming-of-age story about a young prince and the true meaning of kingship and succession. The production team realized that their film's theme should speak to the attendant issues of personal responsibility and that critical point in everyone's life when they must leave their childhood behind and face the world's sometimes harsh realities as an adult.

"For me," says Rob Minkoff, "the primary relationship in the movie is between father and son. This became very clear during the course of one of our first big story meetings. Exploring the characters of Mufasa and Simba helped us dramatize the responsibility theme in a very personal and concrete way."[76]

"Mufasa says it all in the line, 'You must take your place in the circle of life,' " Don notes. "Simba wants to run away and hang out with the lost boys Timon and Pumbaa, but in the end he sees it's his destiny and responsibility to go home and save his father's homeland from tyranny."[77]

"The metaphor of 'How are you responsible for your own community?' or 'How are you responsible in your own family?' " says Roger Allers, "is something that's universal that people can relate to, and I think it's always appropriate."[78] With those converging concepts in mind, they began looking to refine the story in ways that would emphasize the drama of this emerging theme of responsibility.

In many early drafts, once Mufasa died, he was not seen again, and his absence was keenly felt by the storytellers trying to bring Simba's journey to a creatively satisfying conclusion. The team had long been struggling to find a motivation strong enough to make Simba overcome the guilt he feels over his father's death and return to face his past. Since their entire story was based on the bonds between father and son, they came to the conclusion that the answer lay with the final resolution of that relationship.

Taking another page directly from one of their principal inspirations, *Hamlet*, the filmmakers created a stirring sequence in which the lion prince encounters his father's ghost in the clouds high above the African savanna. In this emotional exchange from beyond the grave, Mufasa tells Simba that in forgetting who he is, he has forgotten his father, too. The prospect of dishonoring his father's memory by not taking his place in the circle of life is the one motivating factor powerful enough to convince Simba to leave his guilt and childhood behind to become the lion king he was born to be. It is Simba's supernatural encounter with his father, and its allusion to another tortured young prince destined for greatness, that leads to his own pivotal "To be or not to be?" crisis of conscience. And in this one character-defining moment, and act two curtain, Simba finally chooses to assume this great responsibility and return to the pride lands to claim his rightful place as ruler. Their theme—and, even more to the point, the whole narrative—crystallized for the filmmakers with the creation of this crucial sequence, a story event so powerful that it was destined to grace the one-sheet poster and take its place in the pantheon of great movie moments.

This all-powerful "return of the king" sequence hadn't even been in the film throughout most of its development. "We all decided there needed to be a 'To be or not to be?' scene, and it was the very last scene that was created for the movie," says co-director Rob Minkoff. "After Mufasa visits Simba and leaves, Simba is left wondering what to do. This literally became our 'To be or not to be?' moment. Everything after that became about being as good as that scene."[79]

The new addition gave the film the sequence it needed to deliver on the promise of its responsibility theme, and it tied together all of the converging story elements with which the filmmakers had been grappling for years. "The more you try to make [your film's story] authentic and true and deeper and more resonant," says co-writer Jonathan Roberts, "the more it's going to be like the great myths that endure, that resonate now."[80]

"No one," reiterates Don Hahn, "ever sets out to make a worldwide event or something that influences culture. I don't think you can think about those things or hope to find those things, and in fact, I think if you set out to find those things, you probably fail. As Eric Larson, one of the great Disney animators, used to say, all we really have as crafts-people and filmmakers is sincerity. It's our gift to the audience, and so when you try to put that across, people feel that."[81]

"Later," Roy E. Disney adds, "people would come up and say, 'Why don't you make another one of those?' And I'd say, if we knew how we did it we'd be making them every fifteen minutes!"[82]

The gradual emergence and ultimate delivery of *The Lion King*'s message of personal responsibility, especially as depicted in Simba's encounter with Mufasa's ghost, is the perfect example of the magical alchemy that results from a harmonic convergence of story, character, and theme. The universal appeal and inherent accessibility of issues involving complicated family relationships and the challenge of finding one's place in the world helped turn *The Lion King* into one of the most thematically powerful and emotionally relevant films that Walt Disney Feature Animation had ever produced.

## Show, Don't Tell ································

Why the earlier examination of storyboarding in a book on screen-writing? Because the occasional (okay, frequent) tug-of-war between Disney's writers and story artists illustrates (pun intended) the classic screenwriting maxim: "Show, don't tell." Screenwriters need to write visually—the craft is called *screen*writing—and never put anything down on paper that can't be seen by the camera. Scripts are not required to include camera angles (in fact, producers prefer that such directions be omitted), but writers can certainly narrow any gap between themselves and their directors by trying to paint as vivid a picture on paper as they can. The story is by nature going to evolve (or change outright) the second your collaborators—the director, cinematographer, and production designer—begin to visualize it. Just remember that you are all on the same team; you're all telling the same story. And in those instances of magical alchemy, everyone's voice can be heard because it expresses a singular point of view.

Even though the screenwriter isn't working in as strictly visual a medium as their film's director, cinematographer, or production designer, there are many ways for them to guide or at least inspire their future collaborators in the pages of their script. Rich metaphorical images can help screenwriters paint a vivid picture when dialogue is not enough, especially when there is no other way for the audience to know what a character might be thinking or feeling. This telling imagery can also incorporate descriptions of everything from a location to significant objects to a character's physical attributes.

When we first meet him, Quasimodo helps a bird to fly for the first time, mirroring his own hopes and dreams of taking flight from the bell tower and exploring the outside world. That one poignant moment says more about Quasi's character than an entire page of scripted dialogue ever could, and yet it was created by the screenwriter and can be found in the original script.

In Walt Disney's allegorical masterpiece, *Bambi*, the villain of the piece, "man," is made even more conspicuous by his absence. The audience never actually *sees* a human being. Man and the death and devastation he represents are seen only in the form of a distant campfire, the cataclysmic forest fire it spawns, and those fateful, unforgettable gunshots that claim Bambi's mother. This keeps the audience comfortably ensconced in the natural world of the animals and reinforces the story's contention that man is an intruder in that world, a wanton, destructive force. The significant creative decision to omit human characters was made early on in the process, when the film was squarely in the hands of the story department.

In *Home on the Range*, rustler Alameda Slim keeps his stolen livestock in an abandoned mine honeycombed with labyrinthine passages and hidden chambers. The maze is so complex that the filmmakers even had to color code the corridors so they could block out all the action within their mine "set." The payoff is subtle, but clever: all the mazelike tunnels, rickety bridges, and convoluted spaces reflect Slim's own dark and twisted personality. This, in turn, reinforces his character and the overall story.

## Signs of the Times: Symbolism and Other Recurring Motifs ..........................

*I don't pretend to know anything about art. I make pictures for entertainment, and then the professors tell me what they mean.*

—Walt Disney

As we have seen, a film's theme is home to the story's deeper meaning, and does its best to answer that immortal question, "What's it about?" Since a film is a story and not a sermon, however, the most skillful storytellers do their best to avoid hitting an audience over the head with their preaching, and let them figure out the meaning of life for themselves. As a screenwriter, you can at least help your audience now and again. There are subtle ways to post signs and drop hints of what your story and characters are all about, and that's where the timeless art of symbolism can help you communicate your story's overall message: the hidden and not-so-hidden meanings behind the people, places, and things that populate your film, and the often elusive subtext of your narrative. Like so many other aspects of the screenwriting process, the guiding principle in the use of symbolic elements is "Show, don't tell."

Film is a visual medium, and animation, in a sense, is film in its purest form, since every single thing the audience sees in each frame must be placed there, deliberately, by hand. Although the creation of an animated feature is an ongoing collaboration between screenwriters, directors, story artists, and the animators themselves, writers can begin laying the foundation for symbols and recurring motifs at the scripting stage, and are free to include anything the audience can *see* that will help tell their story. That's just as true of live-action screenplays: if they can see it, you can write it.

With that in mind, there are any number of ways to script visual elements that symbolize story, characters, and theme, and what all three of those elements really mean. From significant objects and locations to representative shapes and colors, virtually anything in a frame of film can contain and convey meaning, whether it's right in the viewer's face or lurking somewhere beneath the surface, working on the audience's subconscious as they absorb and process your story.

Although screenwriters generally go out of their way to avoid scripting anything that might come off as too "on the nose," sometimes a simple and direct approach is the best way to make a point they don't want the audience to miss. An excellent example occurs in *The Lion King*, when Simba symbolically stumbles into his father's gargantuan footprint, and realizes that he has some very big paws to fill in order to meet his destiny as the future lion king. That single symbolic action at once tells something about our young and impetuous lion prince, helps move the story forward, and keenly illustrates the film's overall theme of responsibility. The filmmakers make their point visually and immediately, and it's one of the most compelling moments in the movie.

"The image on the screen needn't be epic and vast and grandiose, although we try to do all those things," says Don Hahn. "One of the most compelling images is the father's paw print and Simba's little paw going into it. It had everything to do with ideas. Rob and Roger had a strong idea about the relationship between a father and a son, and the son taking his father's place. And that became really moving for the audience after a while."[83] The message is clear and driven home forcefully and immediately: Simba has a lot of growing up to do and some very large paw prints to fill. And it is all said without one word of dialogue spoken between them.

Such a scene exemplifies cinematic storytelling in its purest form, and, from a story standpoint, it is the result of the screenwriters, directors, and story artists all granting themselves and each other the freedom to pursue different possibilities, narrative and visual. Such scenes are just one of the many gifts the story artists can bestow on the emerging narrative, and all the more reason for screenwriters to open themselves up to collaboration.

Many symbolic elements are not as readily apparent yet touch the audience on a subconscious level and enhance their experience of the story, even if they're not as aware of it while it is happening. This special brand of symbolism can take the form of anything that conveys additional importance beyond what is obvious to everyone, whether it's a thematically significant object, a carefully chosen color palette, or even the physical characteristics of a character.

## A Rose by Any Other Name Is Just as Symbolic . . . .

In the reel world of *Beauty and the Beast*, a single red rose symbolizes true and unconditional love, just as it has for centuries in the real world (at least in Western culture). When a rose is presented to an arrogant, cruel young prince by a beautiful enchantress disguised as a gnarled old peddler woman, it first represents, in the abstract, the pure love to which he should aspire. You'd be forgiven for thinking that this very obvious use of a traditional symbol is too precious, even trite, for such a sophisticated film. But the enchantress's transformation of the prince into the hideous Beast transforms the symbolic meaning of the rose as well, making it richer and more complex.

Encased in glass and hidden in the dark recesses of the west wing of his lonely palace, the rose slowly dies as the Beast nurses his misanthropy, awaiting the moment when the last petal will fall, imprisoning him forever in his monstrous body—just as the living bloom is itself imprisoned in a bell jar, and the Beast's gentle soul is imprisoned within his ugly body and his embittered heart. In this way the rose represents both the Beast's potential for love (and his desire for it), together with the curse that threatens to prevent his realization of that potential. Once Belle enters the picture, the rose comes to symbolize further the actual love that the beautiful girl shares with the Beast despite his hideous exterior.

With its slowly withering and dropping petals, the rose is also an ingenious visual depiction of a time-honored plot device: the ticking clock. Good screenwriters know that there is nothing like placing a seemingly insurmountable time constraint on their leading characters' main objective to keep audiences on the edges of their seats. In *Beauty and the Beast* the rose as a symbolic timepiece runs like, well, clockwork. We may know intellectually that the Beast has a finite amount of time in which to find a woman who will love him despite his appearance, but it is the motif of the dying rose that makes the passage of time feel urgent and brings this plot point home to us emotionally. With every falling petal, the rose advances the plot, while simultaneously illustrating the film's main moral theme: that we should never base judgments of a person's inner beauty on their outward appearance. This is what filmic storytelling is all about, in the grand tradition of "Show, don't tell." If every element of every film worked as hard as the Beast's multitasking rose, the elusive magical alchemy that we all seek would become not the exception, but the rule.

# I Dream of Freedom: The Genie's Lament ·········

As we have seen, one of *Aladdin*'s most powerful themes deals with the traps in which the various characters find themselves (and, in some cases, *set* for themselves) and the ways in which they escape from them, from the societal norms that bind both Aladdin and Princess Jasmine to seemingly predetermined destinies, to the literal and physical snare that imprisons the Genie: the lamp. In the centuries since the story's creation, the lamp has become symbolic of the tale of Aladdin in general throughout world culture, and co-directors Ron Clements and John Musker realized that, in their film, it could represent their characters' traps and help them present their theme in a very accessible visual way.

The yearning for freedom runs strong throughout *Aladdin*, and we always have the lamp as a visual reminder of the circumstances that keep each of the characters from it. At the end of the film, when all of the characters break free from their traps in one way or another, Aladdin finally wishes for the Genie's freedom—the only possible way in which it could be granted. The gold shackles break apart and fall from the Genie's wrists, forever liberating him from the lamp that has imprisoned him for so long. The Genie's release from the lamp symbolizes the escape each of the characters makes by the story's conclusion, be it a literal or figurative. Jafar, on the other hand, is freed from one trap, serving a Sultan he despises and hopes to overthrow, only to find himself forever trapped (at least until the sequel) in a new one—you guessed it, a lamp.

Once again we have a symbolic element that operates on different and equally important narrative levels. First and most obvious, the lamp is the main plot device—the MacGuffin, to use Alfred Hitchcock's term—an object of desire that sets the entire story into motion. The protagonist and antagonist—Aladdin and Jafar—want the lamp in order to escape the traps in which circumstance has placed them: Aladdin's lowly social station and Jafar's position of servitude beneath a well-meaning but bumbling ruler. In an ironic twist of fate, the one who can make these escapes possible for them, the Genie, is desperate to be rid of the lamp once and for all, for in his case the lamp *is* the trap. Whether the lamp is seen as a prison or the key to getting released from one, it represents the film's central theme of freedom and how you must be true to yourself in order to obtain it. In the process, *Aladdin*'s magic lamp becomes a powerful source of illumination indeed.

## I See What You Mean: The Art of the Motif ........

One of the most effective ways to convey meaning in your story is to symbolically and visually present the audience with the same ideas again and again, whether they're aware of it or not. Such recurring visual motifs, from colors to objects to shapes, can be used to symbolize characters, feelings, and the overall theme of the film. They are among the most basic words in the language of film, and screenwriters should not shy away from presenting the rest of their production team with plenty to translate as their story makes the journey from page to stage.

Recurring imagery can help convey some of your most basic story points, working on the audience's subconscious as the film unfolds before them. The title character in *Mulan*, for example, can be seen gazing into reflective surfaces—a mirror, water, the blade of a sword, and even the dark, glossy marble of her ancestor's tombstones—at key moments throughout the film. This "reflection" motif speaks of her ongoing struggle to truly know and understand the girl she sees in the mirror image, and even the mistaken (and assumed) identity plot points that drive the story. In *Pocahontas*, images of leaves dancing in the wind convey the unseen power of the natural world, or the sacred "Colors of the Wind" of which Pocahontas sings to John Smith in the film's anthem. And in *The Lion King*, the storytellers use a motif of paw prints—specifically big ones—to reinforce the notion that Simba is destined to follow in his father's footsteps and has a lot of growing up to do, in more ways than one, before he can assume the throne.

In *Aladdin* and *The Hunchback of Notre Dame*, recurring color motifs are practically characters unto themselves. Aladdin and the rest of the "good guys" often appear against cool, soothing blue and gold backgrounds. Jafar and his minions, on the other hand, frequently show up with hot, red backgrounds that symbolize the forces of evil. In a similar vein, "*The Hunchback of Notre Dame* was a story about contrasts," producer Don Hahn explains, "the haves versus the have-nots. So we built contrasts into the backgrounds: sunlight versus shadow, warm colors versus cool colors, bright colors versus dark moody colors."[84]

The *Tarzan* storytelling team employed a motif of touching hands and the contrasting shapes and sizes of the fingers to underscore the differences between the ape world and the human world, with the aptly monikered Ape Man himself caught squarely in the middle. "In approaching this project," states *Tarzan* co-director Kevin Lima, "I was trying to find a visual icon that would work on a basic level. I was looking for something that would underscore Tarzan's sense of being alike, yet different from his ape family. The image of touching hands was first conceived as an idea of how Tarzan realizes he and Jane are physically the same. He couldn't look at his own face, but this would give him something that he could look at. The icon of two hands spread through the film and it became a metaphor for Tarzan's search for identity. It first appears when Kala lifts baby Tarzan into her arms, then again at the age of five when he puts his hand up against Kala's and sees that he is different."[85]

At first glance, it might appear that such recurring motifs fall strictly under the purview of the director or production designer in a live-action film, but the filmic journey begins on the page and the attendant responsibility with the writer. Your collaborators behind the camera will certainly use every design element at their disposal to help tell your story, but screenwriters should always think cinematically and write with those potential visuals in mind.

## Collaboration ···································

Filmmaking is a collaborative medium, perhaps the most collaborative of all art forms. It is also widely considered to be a director's medium, something that every aspiring writer (and more than a few professional ones) would do well to consider. In other words, it's not about you, not by a long shot. Sooner or later, it all comes down to collaboration and your ability to incorporate other points of view into your creative process. In an industry in which ego and insecurity can drive interpersonal relationships and have an undue influence on the work itself, that is no small feat.

Even mediums in which writers ostensibly wield more power (television), or appear to have complete creative control (literature and theater), require them to collaborate with their project's many stakeholders, from actors and directors to editors and producers. If you're looking for a writing career that involves only you and your art, you may want to take a long, hard look at poetry, because that's the only field in which you're going to get that kind of autonomy. In the performing arts, collaboration is the order of the day, and that often means compromise. If you know and can accept this going in, you're going to have a much more positive and fruitful creative experience.

"People talk a lot about collaborative moviemaking," says Ted Elliott, co-screenwriter of *Aladdin*, "but I haven't seen moviemaking as collaborative as animation is—ever. This should probably be how all movies are made. You storyboard out the entire movie, you put it all up on reels, you get the voices recorded—and you can see what the movie is going to look like. It's like opening a play for previews before you take it to Broadway. You get a chance to go in and adjust and fix, to polish the dialogue—and, in some cases, completely rethink the structure."[86]

Animation is quite possibly the most collaborative form of filmed entertainment, with every discipline intimately involved with and deeply affected by the work of all the others. This begins with the writers (plural!—just try to find an animated film with a sole screenwriting credit) and continues all the way up to the director's chair, which is usually occupied by a team of at least two people. Other than the initial spark that ignites inside the mind of every artist when they have an idea, there are few if any parts of the creative process that don't involve more than one person. This makes the animated film the perfect vehicle through which to examine the many faces of collaboration.

"I haven't drawn a single character in over thirty years," Walt said in the early sixties. "It's not only that I have no time for it any longer, but I've found development of the stories themselves much more intriguing than drawing. This seems all the more amazing when one considers that each film, no matter how many people have worked on it, has what is called the 'Disney Touch.' The secret is teamwork. Each character is arrived at by group effort. An artist might have a lot of talent and come up with an excellent idea, but if, after it is thoroughly analyzed, the character cannot be adapted and worked with by the group, we discard it."

Many of Disney's best animated features have been written by teams,

> *Whatever we accomplish is due to the combined effort. The organization must be with you or you don't get it done. In my organization there is respect for every individual, and we all have a keen respect for the public.*
>
> —Walt Disney

from Ron Clements and John Musker *(The Little Mermaid)* who collaborated with another writing team, Ted Elliott and Terry Rossio *(Aladdin)* to Chris Sanders and Dean DeBlois *(Lilo & Stitch)*. Disney's many successful writing partnerships are another testament to the studio's belief in a collaborative process that begins with the first keystroke, sometimes before even a single sketch has been drawn.

"Dean and I work together well because we have the same sort of sensibilities but not the same approach," says Chris Sanders. "So Dean writes scenes from a very different angle than I would, and yet when the scene is written it belongs in the same movie, and that keeps things good and fresh. That's the most important thing in any collaboration, that your sensibilities in the end be the same. It means I don't think you can necessarily work with just anybody. There are some people that you just instantly wouldn't work with . . . you wouldn't believe they're making the same movie you are making. And you also don't want to work with somebody who completely agrees with you."[87]

Every writing team's process is different, and there is no one right way or method to collaborate on a screenplay. Some partners literally split their scripts in half and then go off on their own to write their respective

*One rule you should follow in any kind of collaboration is, withhold nothing. It doesn't matter how bad the idea is, you have to say it. What you find in the creative process is that sometimes that stupid idea makes you see it in a completely new perspective and actually allows you to find the great idea. You have to go through that process. If you play it safe and do what you know will work, then you end up doing a retread of something else."[88]*

—Rob Minkoff, director,
The Lion King

scenes. When both partners have completed their assigned scenes, they trade halves and rewrite each other's work. This process continues until both writers are happy with their joint effort, taking advantage of the best these two or more creative minds have to offer.

John Musker and Ron Clements start by putting together an outline before the actual script is written. John then starts at the beginning of the script, and improvises scenes on paper, writing the scenes multiple times, experimenting with different dialogue and business. Then he feeds these pages to Ron who, with editing and adding his own material, begins to construct the script.

"I don't tend to show John anything until a finished draft is done," says Ron Clements, "because I like to get all the way through once from the beginning to end before digging in to evaluate anything. At that point, he reads it, does lots of notes and rewriting and we keep going back and forth until we both think it's ready to show somebody else. It's similar with the rewriting.

"When we bring another writer in, as we did with Rob Edwards on *Treasure Planet*, it's still a similar process. He writes scenes. We rewrite his stuff; he rewrites our stuff. We take a lot of input from everybody. But we try to still keep 'plussing,' which means trying to keep looking for ways to make things work better. Often in the writing, we think of certain things as placeholders until a better idea comes along."[89]

Other teams prefer to write their scripts together from page one, with one writer sitting in front of the computer while the other paces around the writing room, acting out scenes, or otherwise talking through the script. They spitball ideas, perform dialogue exchanges, and argue story points, taking full advantage of being in the same space at the same time for duration of the writing process. Some partners take turns at the keyboard; others don't. The logistics aren't important as long as the process results in a creative dynamic that brings out the best in every writer on the team.

Most successful writing teams consist of partners who truly complement each other, making the team stronger than the individuals would be working alone. One writer might be stronger in terms of plotting or overall story structure while their partner excels at character development and dialogue. The smartest and most secure writing partners embrace their differences in ability, approach, and style, and use them to further enhance their strengths and minimize their weaknesses.

It can be a long and winding road, those 120 pages, and many writers prefer to make the journey with a traveling companion. That's an apt comparison, because ideally your writing partner should be someone with whom you wouldn't mind taking a cross-country trip—on foot, no less. And not only survive, but prosper. It's an intimate relationship, not dissimilar to a marriage, requiring you to share your innermost thoughts and feelings about the world. You need to think long and hard before deciding that you've met "the one," and the partnership requires a lot of care and feeding once you make that commitment. If you do choose to share your journey, the most important thing is to develop a creative process that works for your writing team.

Collaboration might begin with co-writers, but it certainly doesn't end there, especially in the world of animation. In one of the sharpest deviations from live-action production, the screenwriters of animated features must collaborate with an additional layer of creative talent between

> [Together] we made something that not one of us could have done on our own. And that is a very magical thing.[90]
> —Producer Don Hahn on *The Lion King*

themselves and their directors: the story artists. Most writers grow to grudgingly accept the fact that film is a director's medium and learn to live with the fact that the maestro is going to have final say on most creative issues. Working with an entire team of story artists who will visually interpret their script first is new to most screenwriters and can be quite an adjustment for them, especially for those new to the art. But animation is a unique animal, and most Disney screenwriters come to embrace the process when they realize that the constant creative back-and-forth between the story artists, directors, and themselves only makes the story stronger over time. In fact, it is one of the hallmarks of Disney storytelling.

"What we always hope will happen," says Noni White, co-writer of *The Lion King* and *Tarzan*, "is that we write something and give it to the storyboard artists, who will respect what we've written and make it better. Everybody has to be pulling in the same direction. We ended up with a *Tarzan* that is not necessarily what we would have written ourselves, but it was a delight to discover things that we might not have done on our own. It shows the importance of collaboration."[91]

"Everything that goes into a frame," says Chuck Williams, producer, *Brother Bear*, "every bit of dialogue, every gesture, every tree, every rock, the camera angle—is calculated and put there for a reason. That control, coupled with the long period of time it takes to do it, puts a lot of hands into the pot."[92]

The collaboration between screenwriter and director is a fact of life in animation and live-action production (and a necessary evil in the eyes of many directors and screenwriters). The success of that relationship depends largely on the egos, status, and temperaments of the parties involved. We've all heard horror stories about directors who have barred their writers from the set because of their iron fist or their inferiority complex. But there are many more directors who place a high premium on the partnership with their screenwriters, and take full advantage of this valuable creative resource.

Collaboration is a two-way street, and both writers and directors can benefit from their partnership if they maintain the proper respect for each other's craft and the boundaries that surround them. Setting the auteur theory aside (and that's a whole other issue), we may say that writers and directors need each other, and it's as simple as that. "Making an animated film is a collective process, but the directors are the guys who are in charge—the people with the overall vision—and they must provide the glue that holds everything together,"[93] says Don Hahn. Some writers cringe at the thought of taking command of a film set and the attendant responsibility of bringing their script to life. An equal number of directors, however, have never known the fear of staring at a blank page or computer screen. Both artists have a distinct role to play, and they should be there for each other every step of the way, supporting their collaborator and serving the story. "Keep in mind that no one is really right to do this," says Tom Schumacher on animation directors. "No one does what we do. There isn't a school that teaches what we do. The three biggest parts of directing an animated movie are the management of the story process, the management of the artists who make the movie, and the management of the voice talent. To find someone who can do all three is exceedingly rare."[94] A story's journey from page to screen is a long and difficult one, and the writer and director each hold the reins at different points along the way. Both artists should respect the other's point position when they occupy it, and be ready to hand off and receive those reins when the time comes.

Film is a collaborative medium, period. It doesn't matter if it's the writer working with story artists or the director, or the director partnering with the editor or cinematographer. You're seeing a lot of different hearts and minds up their on the screen when you settle into your theater seat. Everyone, no matter what their role in the process and when they play it, has to be willing to put their own ego and point of view aside and support what is best for the story. Ultimately it doesn't matter where an idea comes from or who advocates it; if it's the right thing to do for the story, it's the right thing to do, period.

Said Walt, "Togetherness, for me, means teamwork. In my business of motion pictures and television entertainment, many minds and skilled hands must collaborate. . . . The work seeks to comprehend the spiritual and material needs and yearnings of gregarious humanity. It makes us reflect how completely dependent we are upon one another in our social and commercial life. The more diversified our labors and interest have become in the modern world, the more surely we need to integrate our efforts to justify our individual selves and our civilization."

Since so many aspects of a story begin on the page, sometimes the screenwriter has the most difficult time allowing other people into their process and incorporating different points of view. They have to learn to set aside ego, fear, and insecurity. When the process is working, everyone is acting on behalf of the story, not on their own behalf, and the final product represents the best of everyone, a magical alchemy of diverse artists, disciplines, and points of view. For many, the true joy of motion picture production lies in the reality that it is a shared journey. Creativity is part of the essence of humanity, and coming together to make something from nothing is perhaps the purest possible reflection of who we are.

* * * * * * * * * * * * * * * * * * * * * * * * * * * * * * * * * * * * * * * *

*"Why worry? If you've done the very best you can, worrying won't make it any better. I worry about many things, but not about water over the dam."*

Walt Disney

* * * * * * * * * * * * * * * * * * * * * * * * * * * * * * * * * * * * * *

# Culmination

 "*We must have good stories—we must have them well worked out—we must have people in there who can not only think up ideas but who can carry them through and sell them to the people who have to do with the completion of the thing.*"

Walt Disney

ompleting the first draft of a feature-length screenplay is unquestionably a significant accomplishment in the life of aspiring and professional writers alike. There is nothing more satisfying and fulfilling than typing those two magical words, *Fade Out*. That one moment represents the culmination of months and often years' worth of blood, sweat, toil, and tears, for isn't that really what we're talking about when we use the term *creative juices?* Take the time to reflect on your progress and savor the moment—you've earned it. But don't kid yourself. The journey is far from over. You still have a lot of hard work ahead of you.

Another old screenwriting maxim says, "Scripts aren't written, they're rewritten"—and it's true. You'll do just as much work after your script is "done" (at least after the first draft is done) as you did when your story was just a vague notion floating around in your head. Your story and characters really begin to reveal their secrets and demonstrate their potential when you can finally take a step back and view them as the whole organism that is your finished draft.

You're also going to have to show your work to other people at some point, which opens the door to criticism and compromise, and you'll have to be receptive to these (and have a skin thicker than Dumbo's). Whether you're working with a writing partner, director, or studio, you will inevitably have to learn to incorporate other voices and other points of view into your artistic process. And you'll have to find ways to be happy and creatively satisfied with the shared vision that results from compromise. It's just one of the emotional costs of doing business in the field of popular entertainment.

And so we embark on the culmination of this journey, your own personal act three, which will bring your story to an end. We'll examine both personal and professional aspects of the post-draft phase of screen storytelling and beyond, including rewriting, and its more aggressive sibling, reconcepting; reacting to criticism; and living and working as an artist. It will be a hero's journey, with the hardest battles, moments of darkest despair, and ultimate rewards leading to the satisfying culmination of all your efforts.

## Writing Is Rewriting . . . or Starting Over Entirely!

You have a working draft of your script. The terror of the blank page or computer screen is past, at the very least. As the protagonist you are writing about inevitably must too, you have reached a point of no return on your own journey of discovery. You're much closer to your final destination, and the attendant reward, than you are to the starting point in your ordinary world. Your ultimate goal is a rock-solid final draft, a screenplay that is as ready to shoot as you can possibly make it. And the only way you're going to accomplish this is by re-evaluating, refining, and rewriting your script.

Rewrites are different for everyone. Many successful writers feel they do their best work when they're rewriting. The story becomes clearer to them; the characters feel more like old friends than new acquaintances; and strong themes begin to emerge, even if they weren't there—or if the writers didn't realize they were there—in the first draft or two. Rewriting enables them to see holes in the plot, eliminate contradictions and inconsistencies in character, polish dialogue, recognize symbolic and thematic patterns, and make each of these story elements stronger.

Other writers believe they have gotten as close to the mark as they could in their first drafts, and do minimal rewriting, even if those first drafts might take that much longer to finish. They capture what they see in their mind's eye and get it on paper in one burst of creative energy, then stand back, and say, "That's it."

Keep in mind that for every writer who has supposedly cranked out a script over a weekend, there are a dozen others who have taken years to get their screenplays as close to perfect as they possibly could. In each case, that particular writer's way was the only way for them to work. The point is that every writer is different, and so is every writer's process. You should just do what feels right for you and, more to the point, your story. The key is to maintain faith in your story, and let that belief drive your script to completion. Be aware that it might mean drastically changing or eliminating story and character elements over which you may have spent months or years agonizing. "Almost all our movies—*Beauty and the Beast, The Rescuers Down Under* and *Aladdin*," reveals Peter Schneider, former president of Feature Animation, "about a year and

> *I always say that when you make a film there is a film that everybody thinks you're making and then, as the film starts being made, it takes on a life of its own. It's like spaghetti sauce. You have all these ingredients and you've got the recipe, but you really don't know what it's going to taste like until it's sat in the refrigerator overnight.*[95]
> —Lisa Keene, Character design/visual development, *The Lion King*

a half before they're released, we throw everything out and we start again."[96] The storytellers at Feature Animation have lived in such a culture of change since the late 1930s. It is a tradition that began with no less a perfectionist than Walt Disney himself.

## Building a Better Puppet ●●●●●●●●●●●●●●●●●●●●●●●●

The commitment to excellence takes conviction, in both the talent and the material, and courage, neither of which is in abundant supply in the executive suite at most Hollywood studios. But Walt Disney set a very different precedent, and the studio that bears his name continues to cultivate an environment in which their artists can muster the self-assurance to say, "This isn't working." It can get a little expensive and very frustrating, for both the "show" people and the "business" people, but the players on both sides know that this approach pays off in the long run. Both history and experience have shown that more than one Disney classic owes its existence to its creators' willingness to call for a do-over.

Everyone working on *Pinocchio* wanted to surpass *Snow White*, artistically and commercially. But as production commenced, Walt felt that the new film lacked the warmth and appeal—the heart—of his first animated feature. More to the point, he felt their sophomore effort lacked an engaging central character, and so he halted production, placing *Pinocchio* on an indefinite hiatus after an enormous outlay of time and money, neither of which were in plentiful supply at the time.

Their titular star, "little woodenhead" himself, didn't possess nearly the same sympathetic qualities that had made Snow White such an appealing and accessible heroine. Walt knew that since Pinocchio would be the conduit through which viewers experienced the story, they had to truly care about the puppet. He had to be someone with whom an audience would want to spend eighty minutes.

Walt and his story team performed some major surgery on

Pinocchio's character to make him more user-friendly. In early treatments, Pinocchio was originally a borderline delinquent who deliberately looked for trouble. The filmmakers remade him into more of a wide-eyed innocent abroad, easily swayed by peer pressure and other bad influences. On the visual side, they made Pinocchio softer, less angular and more rounded, and closer in appearance to a real boy. Even Pinocchio's conscience, Jiminy Cricket, got a facelift. Early concepts had him looking much more realistic and overtly insectlike. He was transformed into the anthropomorphized and endearing character we know and love today. Once the characters' reformation was complete, the film resumed production and went on to become one of Walt's crowning achievements.

Mothballing *Pinocchio*, even temporarily, took the heart and nerve to halt production and thus delay any revenue from the film until the story and characters were absolutely right. All of this took place at a time when The Walt Disney Company was not the heavily diversified, multinational conglomerate that it is today. Consumer products as a source of income did not play nearly as big a role as they do now, and there were no television or theme park divisions to pick up the slack when the film studio wasn't bringing in much revenue. It was a bold and courageous move, and illustrated Walt's commitment to getting a story absolutely right before his artists committed it to paper, let alone celluloid.

## The Kindest Cut of All ··························

There's still another old screenwriting maxim that says, "When in doubt, cut it out." If you're lucky, that might refer to some dialogue, a minor character, or perhaps a scene that isn't working. At Walt Disney Feature Animation, the creative element in question is rarely as simple as this, giving this golden rule of screenwriting a schedule-skewering, budget-busting addendum: "When in doubt, throw it out—*all* of it!"

Some of their processes may be different from those of an individual screenwriter, but the filmmakers at Feature Animation keep rewriting until their stories are absolutely right, even if that means making wholesale changes long after the film has gotten its green light and gone into production. Studio executives from Walt Disney himself on down have given them that mandate and the confidence it inspires. The tradition of the Studio's willingness to send film projects back into development was destined to live on during the second golden age of Disney animation.

*Aladdin* made it all the way to the story-reel stage, when storyboards are filmed and combined with a scratch track of rough dialogue and temporary music. Jeffrey Katzenberg, then head of The Walt Disney Studios, wasn't entirely pleased with what he saw and decided that co-directors Ron Clements and John Musker should start over. "*Aladdin* had a tortured life," says John. "It was completely storyboarded at one point, but crashed and burned, so we had to start over.

"Howard [Ashman] had some controversial things in his treatment," John continues. "His version of the Genie was sort of a Fats Waller kind of character. The princess was a comic character who only cared about her hair and nails, and was very materialistic, while the real heroine was a female sidekick of Aladdin's, a real tomboy, kind of a true-blue type. She was part of his little street gang and they ultimately fell in love, and Aladdin never got involved with the princess."[97]

"The original story was sort of a winning-the-lottery kind of thing," his co-writer and co-director Ron Clements adds. "When we got into it, particularly coming in at the end of the nineteen-eighties, it seemed like an Eighties 'greed is good' movie. Like having anything you could wish for would be about the greatest thing in the world and having that taken away from you is bad, but getting it back is great. We didn't really want that to be the message of the movie. We tried to put a spin on it. Like having anything you could wish for may *seem* like the greatest thing in the world. But things are never quite what they seem."[98]

"[The studio] said 'Let's do something Aladdin-ish,' " says John. " 'You know, something Arabian Nights-y.' We really responded to *Aladdin* and there were elements of Howard's treatment that we wanted to go back to, especially some of the songs. So we used elements of Howard's treatment, adapted some things, and then introduced our own ideas."[99]

Under John and Ron's patient direction (and re-direction), *Aladdin* continued its metamorphosis. "In the early screenings," says John, "we played him a little bit younger and he had a mother in the story. We reconceived the character, and Aladdin became an orphan living by his wits on the street. And in the design he became more athletic-looking, more filled out, more of a young leading man, more of a teen-hunk version than before. He became seventeen to eighteen rather than thirteen, and the whole romance story was built up more."[100]

In addition to eliminating his mother, the writers also removed Aladdin's tomboyish female friend, clearing the way for him to romance Princess Jasmine, who didn't have much contact with the hero in the early version. Clements and Musker refashioned *Aladdin*—with the help of live-action screenwriters Ted Elliott and Terry Rossio, who would go on to co-write *The Mask of Zorro, Shrek,* and *Pirates of the Caribbean: The Curse of the Black Pearl*—into a romance between hopelessly star-crossed lovers set against the backdrop of a rollicking action-adventure story. The original story, like many of the fairy tales upon which Disney films are based, features a boy and a girl playing traditional and narrowly defined roles. But Clements and Musker were determined to take *Aladdin* far beyond the familiar paradigm of boy meets girl, boy loses girl, boy gets girl. The story they had in mind had a lot to say about traditional male and female roles in society—and modern society, to boot, even though *Aladdin* is set in the ancient Middle East.

As they hoped that Aladdin would represent a new kind of Disney hero, Clements, Musker, and company similarly had no intention of allowing Princess Jasmine to become the traditional damsel in distress. Instead, Jasmine continued the process of evolution that began with Ariel and continued with Belle, creating a new court of Disney Princesses who could inspire and enlighten young girls in addition to determining their Halloween costumes and bedroom decor. Ted Elliot and Terry Rossio's rewrites helped define her independence. Their line for her, "I am not a prize to be won!" crystallized her strong will.

In an early incarnation of the story, Jasmine was bound by law to marry before her sixteenth birthday. The team quickly realized that such a plot point wouldn't send the greatest message to all the unmarried fifteen-year-olds in the world, and decided to dodge the issue by having the Sultan say things like, "Jasmine, the law says you must be married to a prince by your next birthday." Now that Aladdin was being played older, it would at least appear that both were of marrying age even if this point wasn't explicitly stated. This revised "condition" added something of a ticking clock to the story, at least from Jasmine's point of view, and also vastly reduced the pool of suitors from which she could choose. And that is the operative word: *choose*. Like Ariel and Belle before her, Princess Jasmine has definite opinions on what she wants to do with her life, including whom she will marry, and when.

Jasmine makes her displeasure with the marriage law known to her father, the Sultan, offering fiery displays of independence, rebellion, and strength throughout the film. The Sultan thinks he's off the hook when Jasmine does indeed fall for Prince Ali Ababwa (really Aladdin in an elaborate disguise created for him by the Genie). Yet it is not the royal trappings that attract Jasmine to Prince Ali, but Aladdin's strength, confidence, and inner worth shining through the subterfuge. Jasmine is understandably outraged when she discovers the truth, not because Aladdin isn't really a prince, but because he has lied to her and failed to trust her capacity to love him for himself.

In the end, Aladdin is forced to shed the costume and be himself, and that is what ultimately wins him the heart and hand of Jasmine. With all the cards on the table, Jasmine, in turn, winds up choosing Aladdin. Moreover, he doesn't rescue her or "select" her because she is the fairest in the land or has the correct shoe size. Jasmine makes her own choice precisely because Aladdin has learned that it is better to be himself than to masquerade as a false prince. With both characters firmly in charge of their own identities and destinies, they truly can live happily ever after, and they've earned the right to.

Clements and Musker transformed the story of *Aladdin* from an ancient Arabic fable into a postmodern animated action adventure-romantic comedy filled with sensitive males, empowered females, and a pop culture–riffing Genie who at various times assumes the identity of Woody Allen, Jack Nicholson, and Ed Sullivan, with plenty of show tunes and 1930s-style jazz numbers thrown in.

Today *Aladdin* stands as one of the highest-grossing Disney animated films of all time, and remains one of the most critically acclaimed, as well. It's hard for anyone to imagine the film any other way than the version seen on the screen—anyone other than Ron Clements, John Musker, and the creative team they led through the hell of seeing their entire story vaporized, that is. Neither the filmmakers nor moviegoers around the world will ever know how the film might have fared in its original form. The success of their page-one rewriting (and, in many cases, reconcepting), is a testament to the sheer power of confidence and maintaining the faith to shoulder on, even when it looks as though none of your ideas is working.

The studio continues to give its artists the freedom, and the attendant time and money, to keep rewriting and refining a story until it is as good as it can possibly be. *Kingdom of the Sun*, an epic tale of love and mistaken identity set in an ancient South American Indian civilization, had the most painful birth of any of the Disney animated features. It began life as a full-blown musical with six songs composed by Sting. At one point during this creatively gut-wrenching process, the studio contemplated throwing out *all* of Sting's compositions before settling for a small handful of songs. Also reconcepted were a *Prince and the Pauper*–like mistaken identity aspect of the story, the romantic subplot, and the film's overall epic quality. The story was vastly simplified and settled into the same light comedic vein as *Aladdin* and *Hercules*. The project flirted with another title, *Kingdom in the Sun* (story issues are examined down to the last word), before taking into account the film's new tone and style and selecting its final title. *The Emperor's New Groove* became a commercial and critical success; not a home run by any means, but a solid double.

It should come as no surprise that screenwriters need to have more confidence than the average person. How else could they commit months or years of their lives to a project with no guarantee of its ever being seen by one pair of Hollywood eyes much less those of millions of moviegoers? There is no promise of financial remuneration. Screenwriters don't even know if what they're working on will ever be produced. All they have to get themselves through those 120 pages—as many times as it takes—is an unshakable faith in themselves and in their material.

Confidence will buy you the time you'll need to do your best work. In fact, all you have is time. No one will ever really know how long it took you to write your script, especially if it's a spec script, so take all the time and as many drafts you need. Even if it's a studio assignment with a firm deadline,

> When we consider a new project, we really study it—not just the surface idea, but everything about it. And when we go into that new project, we believe in it all the way. We have confidence in our ability to do it right. And we work hard to do the best possible job.
>
> —Walt Disney

they're never going to know how many hours per day or how many passes went into the first draft they see. Write until it's right, and don't stop until you know you've reached that point. And you *will* know. Your creative instincts will let you know when there is nothing further that you can do to better your script. How could it be otherwise? No one knows your story better than you do, and you have internalized much of that information, whether you know it or not. It doesn't matter if it takes you one draft or one hundred; you should write and rewrite your script until you can honestly say to yourself, "This is exactly what I set out to do with my story." Writers in any medium owe themselves permission to do the same. They just might give the world its next *Lion King*.

## Make It Better, Not Different ....................

*"There's a difference between 'plussing' and arbitrarily changing. We usually feel pretty confident about what we're trying to do, but less confident about whether we're doing it the best that it can be done. Or even whether or not we're communicating what we think we are. We're always looking for a better idea."*[101]

Ron Clements

The French poet Paul Valéry is often quoted as saying, "A poem is never finished, only abandoned." Picasso is said to have made the same remark about painting. Both attributions are probably apocryphal, but director George Lucas really did once say that films are never finished, only abandoned, and the same is certainly true for screenplays. Perhaps all artists feel this way about their work, which would explain why the insight is so often repeated.

You could rewrite forever if you wanted to, always looking to make it just a little bit better. The big question is whether you really are making it better, or just different. That risk is real enough when it's just you and a computer monitor. Throw in a collaborator or two, a small army of studio executives, and, eventually, test audiences, and the potential exists to tinker your story into bland mediocrity.

The only way to combat this threat is to always put the story first. That's not as easy as it sounds. It's a fact of creative life that some people just want their voices to be heard and their voices represented in the script. Sometimes a more powerful collaborator or a creative executive who just wants to leave their mark on a project will insist on a change that not only doesn't make a film better but actually makes it worse. The thought of being able to point at something, anything, on a movie screen and tell friends and family, "I did that," is a powerful temptation that sometimes leads even the purest of artistic hearts to put ego ahead of story.

Ego is a double-edged sword, however, and it is more than happy to cut both ways. More often than not, your collaborators, sounding boards, and studio executives *are* putting the story first, and they are bound to have good ideas of their own every once in a while. And yes, as hard as it may be to accept or believe, some of those ideas are going to be better than yours. Unfortunately, artists' insecurities, or their egos, can lead them to cling to their own ideas at any cost, even when it becomes clear that their stubborn refusal to embrace a better idea is hurting their film. A smart writer or director will happily use an idea that will better their film, regardless of where it came from.

> There's an attitude in animation. "How can I make this film better?" Wherever a good idea comes from—as long as it's a good idea—let's use it.[102]
> —Terry Rossio,
> co-screenwriter, *Aladdin*

## Stop Me If You've Heard This Before ·············

At some point, you're going to have to send your script out into the world to be read—and judged—by an agent, a studio, or even just a small group of friends whose taste and opinions you respect and trust. You're also going to have to be open to their feedback, or "notes," as they say in the industry. They all loved the wisecracking action hero and the unforeseen reversal of fortune at the end of act two, but not one of them bought your Hitchcockian twist ending and suggested that you might have seen *The Sixth Sense* one too many times. If more than a few readers tell you they don't understand or accept something in your script, you would do well to take their "consensus of confusion" into consideration. Something might make perfect sense and work for *you*, but if the majority of people that read your script gives you the same note, you need to concede that there might be a problem and rethink that part of your story. Don't worry, you're not betraying your artistic principles by responding to your own little, informal "focus groups." Ultimately you are writing this for an audience, not your own amusement, and you should listen to them while you still have the chance. Once your story gets up there on the big screen, it's too late.

"One of the biggest issues we had to deal with," says Chris Sanders about the development of *Lilo & Stitch*, "was, why was everybody chasing Stitch?" In the original outline as pitched to the studio, Stitch was the leader of an alien criminal gang that was guilty of hooliganism. "They committed vandalism, wrecked street signs, etcetera," recalls Chris, "and one member of the gang, Jumba, had been captured and was going to be used to track down Stitch, who would then be the lynchpin by which the rest of the gang would be gathered. But both Tom [Schumacher] and Peter [Schneider] thought this didn't seem like a big enough reason for them to go after Stitch."[103] Sanders and company were a good year into the production at this point. Then a

> *My favorite part of the process is when you start servicing the movie. Think of your film like a big locomotive. First, it's sitting on the tracks and you start pushing it. You're making chugging sounds and it gets easier and easier to push. Eventually, you're running alongside, servicing it. It will tell you what it needs, and what it doesn't. It will reject things, it will want things. It becomes a living organism and I love that part the best. The more things we tear off of it and have to change out, the happier I get.[104]*
>
> —Chris Sanders

meeting occurred where two comments changed the course of the film. "Tom said, 'I love this character, I think this is a great movie. I don't get the gang.' Well, this was something he had said a year before."[105]

Then Roy E. Disney queried something that Chris thought was very important. "I liked Stitch when I thought he was a baby," Roy told Chris, "but when I learned at the end of the movie that he was middle-aged, I didn't like him as well." At that meeting, says Chris, "The whole movie changed course. We could have chosen to battle them on those points and say, 'Okay, we'll deal with them,' but I had been hearing those things for about a year and I knew that we weren't going to work it out. So what we did was we got rid of the gang in that meeting. Right there, in that meeting."[106] It's one thing to consider and accept a drastic change in a story, it's another to decide a different direction to pursue. The filmmakers needed to rethink the vital "What if . . . ?" question.

"We tried having Stitch steal a time machine or an important military code, or the key to some dangerous device," Chris recalls. "The problem with all of these things was that it was an external reason for them to go looking for Stitch. We thought we had to literally attach this thing of value that he had stolen to Stitch to make people go after him. But I said we needed to find a way to make people go after him just because he's Stitch. Then we can lose the gang, lose all of the machinery. Unfortunately, we would also lose two or three sequences where we had maintained the gang. We had already gone to visit them on the planet they were hiding out on.

"Everybody got really quiet and then someone said 'What if . . . they carry him around in a jar? We see guys with Hazmat suits move him, they stick him with needles, they act almost like he's a virus. What if he *was* a virus, or the equivalent of a virus? What is the equivalent of a virus? And I said out loud: a genetic mutation. And that would be a reason to chase him—just because he *is* one. And it would also somewhat justify why they would be carrying him around in a little closed jar—because they really treat him—more like a virus than a criminal in the very beginning.

"That's one of the strange things about the movie," Chris says. "The movie seemed to be waiting for that change the whole time. The room was dead quiet because this was an immense change to suggest midway through the process. Nobody moved. It was an absolutely silent room and then Tom looked at me and nodded and said, 'Let's do this.' But what would we do? Jumba is no longer the gang member. Then Dean said, maybe he's the scientist that made him. Okay, good, now Jumba's still there. We'll just put a lab coat on him and change his dialogue. Then the

> If one person tells you, "I didn't get this," then you should take note of that and if you don't agree, move on. However, if two to three people tell you that over the course of time, you should start listening, because that means that something's wrong with the story and you just can't ignore that.[107]
> —Chris Sanders, co–writer-director, *Lilo & Stitch*

only real change we had to make was, find another person to go after Stitch at the end. So is there anybody at that point who's angry at Stitch? And we thought, well, yeah, there's the guy who captained the prison ship that Stitch got away from. He probably has an axe to grind. Maybe he's the guy who shows up in the end."[108] As the brainstorming continued, point after point fell into place, the result of a now-solid plot structure brought about by an initial consensus of confusion.

So, how do you know something is better and not just different? Such certainty is one of those elements of magical alchemy, and has more to do with intuition than intellect. More often than not, you'll experience that exhilarating jolt of electricity that tells you when you've nailed something. You're so in tune with your story that you will know instinctively what's right for it when you see or hear it. A better idea—the right idea—literally takes your breath away, and there is no mistaking it. And once your mind has been opened to it, there's no going back.

A deceptively simple notion can change the course of an entire film. The producers of *Brother Bear* encountered just such an offhand suggestion that made their film vastly different from what they had envisioned, and much, much better. Originally, the character of Kenai (voiced by Joaquin Phoenix), upon his transformation into a bear, partnered up with an older and much bigger bruin named Grizz (Michael Clark Duncan), who showed him the ropes of the animal world. Both characters were strong and interacted well together, but the story just wasn't jelling. Kenai just couldn't learn what he needed to learn from another older-brother figure, even one that happened to be a grizzly bear.

Then the production team experienced an epiphany as great as the transformation Kenai undergoes in their story. "What if we made Grizz a bear cub?" someone casually asked during a story meeting. The filmmakers could literally feel the atmosphere change in the story room, and in that instant they knew—they *felt*—that this was the way to go. And so Koda, voiced by young Jeremy Suarez, was born.

It is out of just such seemingly inconsequential moments that fresh, new ideas can emerge and change the course of your entire story. As the makers of *Brother Bear* learned firsthand, you have to be willing to endure a sometimes grueling discovery process and make some very painful decisions to get there. Replacing Grizz with Koda was one of them.

"The directors wanted to make sure that it was better," says Leo Chu, vice president of Creative Affairs, "more emotional, and more entertaining, and not just different. A lot of times when you're in constant rewriting mode, sometimes just because something is new and different, it becomes exciting, but it's a question of recognizing that it's a better idea."[109]

Now, all of a sudden, Kenai is the older brother for the first time. He is responsible for little Koda in ways he cannot comprehend until the end of act two when he learns Koda's mother is the bear he killed to avenge the death of his own older brother, Sitka. The filmmaker's notion of seeing the world through another's eyes began to take on a new and compelling form, one that enabled the rest of their story to fall into place.

Co-directors Aaron Blaise and Bob Walker felt they had a wonderful character in Grizz, and didn't want to lose Michael Clark Duncan's vocal performance. Since Kenai needed to take most of his journey alone with Koda in order to serve the story, Grizz became Tug, the de facto leader of the bears who have gathered together at the salmon run. The writers relegated him to bit-player status, and yet Tug is still a commanding and memorable presence in the film. The reconception of his character cleared the way for Koda to come in, and enabled all the other story elements to fall into place.

"The plot changed and the characters changed throughout," says Chuck Williams, producer, *Brother Bear*. "I think that's part of the collaborative process. There is always a big fear when two different ideas are put on the table. You've invested so much in one idea that—unless the other idea is really overwhelmingly better, you really should try to stick to it. Nevertheless, you have to be able to check your ego at the door to hear someone else's point of view, even if it's not what you saw, what you envisioned. It's especially hard on the person who came up with the original idea. It's just human nature to like your idea better than anything else. It's a tricky thing. You have to be able to step back and let the idea just sort of live or die and breathe. Just give it time for that."[110]

There's no question that changing an older mentor figure—Grizz—into a younger brother in need of guidance—Koda—made *Brother Bear* a very different movie, but the filmmakers also instinctively knew that the change made it a much *better* movie in the process. The trick is to have the ability to put aside your own preconceptions and point of view and entertain different and often radical ideas. You must then also have faith that your own creative instincts will let you know when one of those ideas is truly better than anything you have, and you must feel secure enough to make the changes that will improve your story.

## Fight For Your Write ····························

There are times, however, when making it "better" actually means fighting to keep it as it is. While producers and studio executives can often make valuable creative contributions, screenwriters who have put their heart and soul into the story should not just randomly accept changes they don't believe will truly strengthen their film.

Writer-director Ron Clements encountered such a situation while making *The Little Mermaid*. "There were huge arguments on various things. There were a lot of things one of the top studio executives wanted to do and some of them made the film better but there were also a lot of things we argued about. One of his suggestions was to cut the song 'Part of your World.' We invited students from a local elementary school to view a fairly early-stage black-and-white version of the song and some of the students squirmed and got restless during that sequence."[111] This has long been a generally accepted sign that a scene or sequence wasn't working. But Ariel supervising animator Glen Keane talked the executive team into leaving it in the film for one more test screening. Sure enough, "at the next screening," Ron recalls, "there was color and they didn't squirm any more. Arguing is a good thing—and when taking a stronger stand, you might discover something you didn't notice before."[112]

## Don't Be Afraid of Fear ........................

There are a number of spirit-sapping forces out there that can spook even the most self-assured of journeyman storytellers. Confidence will take you a long way, but, at some point, its stronger and more aggressive cousin, courage, is going to have to take over if you hope to continue on your path. That's not to say that fear is a bad thing. Far from it. Fear can be a very useful motivator and even a source of power. In fact, longtime lead animator Glen Keane handed out a copy of the book, *Art and Fear: Observations on the Perils (and Rewards) of Artmaking* by David Bayles and Ted Orland, to key collaborators on his upcoming directorial debut, *Rapunzel Unbraided*. The book argues that fear is an indispensable tool for anyone engaged in an artistic pursuit. In fact, fear of a project is the surest and most direct sign that you should tackle it. Fear will keep everyone from resting on his or her laurels. Walt would approve.

Now, the world we've been exploring so far is populated by good-natured mice and flying elephants, so what is there to be afraid of? Quite a bit, as it turns out. There are a number of mentally and emotionally destructive things that people typically try to avoid in life, all of which are just part of the daily routine in the entertainment industry. These include criticism, rejection, failure, the prospect of watching something that is a part of you—your screenplay—evaporate right in front of your eyes, and the fear of all those things. While it might take a strong ego to climb into the same ring with these formidable opponents, only the most courageous are able to stare them down again and again and still come back for more. And when you're one of those "sensitive creative types," that's much easier said than done.

One of the things all these more negative aspects of the business have in common is exposure, specifically exposing yourself and your work to anyone outside your comfort zone. Other than the occasional (or more likely frequent) crisis of confidence, there's not much that can truly threaten you when you are alone with your work. Writing partners and the friends and family members you use as sounding boards are on your side, so even they aren't much of a threat to sense of security. The first outside entity that will have a definite opinion on your work and a potential effect on your career: the studio.

## The Studio, or, the Pluses and Minuses of "Entertainment by Committee" ·················

We've already seen some of the forms of collaboration in both live-action and animation screenwriting, and the trust it takes to work as part of a writing team. There is one creative partnership that everyone on a project shares: the collaboration with the studio, and that relationship takes a lot more than confidence. Sharing your innermost thoughts and feelings with a writing partner or two within the safe confines of your work space is one thing, but baring your heart and soul in the form of a screenplay for all the corporate world to see takes nothing less than raw courage.

During the golden age of animation, Walt Disney *was* the studio, and even with all the collaboration that took place, the films ultimately represented his vision. After Walt died, the studio continued to play an active role in the development and production of the animated films, although the infamous question, "What would Walt do?" was asked far too often in the decade after his death. Instead of marching forward into the future and blazing new ground as their founder would most certainly have done, the studio executives tried a little too hard to recapture the Disney magic that had always been uniquely Walt's. It would be almost two decades before they would finally learn that the solution to the studio's problems lay in finding and nurturing a new voice or voices to speak to a new generation of moviegoers who considered Disney to be hopelessly out of touch with mainstream audiences. The studio's hands-on approach led to something of an "entertainment by committee" philosophy that endures today.

"It worked for a while," says Roy E. Disney on the early post-Walt years. "Right after Walt died, we sort of constituted a 'group of seven,' if you want to call it that, in which I was one of the seven. We were all reading each other's scripts. Then we'd send all our stuff around to everybody and write our responses. The 'creative committee' actually did work for a while. *The Love Bug* happened

> I think if there's any part I've played . . . the vital part is coordinating these talents, and encouraging these talents, and carrying them down a certain line. It's like pulling together a big orchestra. They're all individually very talented. I have an organization of people who are really specialists. You can't match them anywhere in the world for what they can do. But they all need to be pulled together, and that's my job.
>
> —Walt Disney

that way, for instance. You wouldn't believe the transition it made from the first script to what it ultimately became. There were some others that evolved through the same process. Live-action, animation—everything we did was subjected to that.

"As time went by," Roy continues, "people began saying, 'That's mine—keep out of my territory,' a little more often than they had in the beginning. Everybody was just baffled by the fact that there was no Walt, you know, because he was everybody's daddy and everybody's critic and the final answer to everything. If we can't decide on this ourselves, what would Walt think? And when you don't have that, it's a real problem."[113]

"Entertainment by committee." Never has a studio management style so polarized the creative community. Although that notorious phrase is commonly used to criticize Hollywood's tendency to aim its product to the lowest common denominator, at Feature Animation "the process," as it has come to be called, is held in much higher regard—by the "show" people as well as the "business" people—and actually appears to work more often than not.

A story needs to be as right as it can be before the studio commits it to animation. Animation producers can't afford to spend the time it takes to animate a scene only to discover that it doesn't work. That's why animated features spend such a long time in development. Naturally the studio wants to be intimately involved every step of the way, for both financial and artistic reasons. After all, these films are going to bear the name *Walt Disney*, and that means a great deal to everyone associated with the animated features.

In fact, one of the main reasons the studio brass plays such an active role is its responsibility for carrying on the Disney tradition. The filmmakers have a very important legacy left by Walt and his artists to live up to, and a sterling reputation to protect. Disney's executives and storytellers live and work in the present, but not without taking frequent looks over their shoulder at the past, and rightfully so; they're carrying a lot of artistic responsibility on their shoulders.

"Ah, the Disney tradition," says Roy. "We are who we are, and we understand that there's an expectation there, and, in fact, the expectations can be a burden if you let them. But the way I've always put it is that we need to understand our history—not because we need to be imitative of it, not to oppress our judgment of what we're doing in any way. We just need to know how bloody goddamn good [the early animated features] were and think of ourselves as having to be that good, too. From that point of view, the history of the place is enormously valuable and no place else has that."[114]

Disney's past is always with us, but there is also the future to consider. No one wants the company to become a museum, which is what it would essentially be if the studio stopped creating new characters and telling new stories. Beyond the film world, there are television channels, theme parks, and consumer products to consider, and new animated properties lead to fresh content for each one of these ancillary markets. Everything Disney does is built on that which has come before, and the current regime is determined to make their projects worthy of the past while reinforcing the foundation for future generations of Disney storytellers.

This creative partnership between filmmakers and their studio executives benefits projects in the long run. Unlike the producers, writers, and directors, who are embroiled in one project at any given time, executives can retain an objectivity that enables them to bring fresh eyes to story and production issues. They can help the creative talent look at their material in new ways, and offer different perspectives on challenges that the production team has been living with every day for months on end. They can be the most valuable kind of sounding board, provided filmmakers can remain open to—and not threatened by—new ideas.

New and aspiring writers aren't going to have many options when it comes to dealing with a studio. On the contrary, most newcomers consider themselves lucky to be in the same room with studio people, because it's a sign of at least some measure of success. Be open to what they have to say, even if you don't like everything you hear (and you probably won't).

You're going to have to work *with* them if you'd like to continue working *for* them. That's why it's important to remember that you're on the same team, working toward the same end: a great movie. So, before you start screaming about how studio execs are "violating your artistic integrity" or "ruining your story," try to remember what they bring to the process and know that they want to help you tell the best possible story. You can learn a lot from them, and you don't want to risk getting replaced because you were unable or unwilling to collaborate and, yes, compromise, with the studio.

## Giving Rejection the Slip ........................

Anyone who decides to pursue a vocation in show business has chosen one of the most difficult career paths imaginable. It is a life fraught with competition, rejection, criticism, and failure, much more so than many other professional pursuits. There are countless, vastly different fields within the industry, but that's one thing they all have in common. Show business in general, and the movie industry in particular, are equal-opportunity rejecters.

Artistic sensitivity is a double-edged sword. Criticism and rejection generally have more serious

> It is good to have a failure while you're young because it teaches you so much. For one thing it makes you aware that such a thing can happen to anybody, and once you've lived through the worst, you're never quite as vulnerable afterward.
>
> —Walt Disney

effects on sensitive, artistic types, those emotionally vulnerable people who are putting themselves on display in their work for all the world to see and pass judgment on. The rub, of course, is that if you are hoping to pursue a career in the arts, it greatly helps to *be* such an emotionally vulnerable and sensitive artistic type. "I have been up against tough competition all my life," said Walt. "I wouldn't know how to get along without it. All the adversity I've had in my life, all my troubles and obstacles, have strengthened me. You many not realize it when it happens, but a kick in the teeth may be the best thing in the world for you."

An aspiring writer needs to be steadfast in the pursuit of a dream: no one is going to come to you and ask you to be a writer. A working writer needs to be dedicated to the craft once that first dream has been realized. What they share is a burning desire to see their stories on the big screen, and it has to be strong enough to carry them through the dark times—and there will be dark times.

## What's *My* Motivation ··························

Screenplays can take months and often years to write. The films made from those scripts can take years to make as well—and, in the case of animated features, quite a few of them. You can imagine how true and absolute a filmmaker's belief in the material must be in order to stay so committed to it for such considerable lengths of time. And with years of people's lives and tens (or even hundreds) of millions of dollars at stake, the artists primarily responsible for telling the story, both on paper and on film, had better believe in it more than anybody.

The power of motivation is evident on an organizational level as well. Many of Disney's most memorable animated features had lengthy histories. Both *Alice in Wonderland* and *Peter Pan* are prime examples of projects with long gestations, but are now considered bona fide classics, a testament to Walt's unwavering belief in and passion for the stories on which they are based. Even *The Little Mermaid*, the film that kicked off Disney Feature Animation's second golden age, had been kicking around the studio since its early years; Walt had long been interested in bringing one of Hans Christian Andersen's classic tales to life. If the passion behind a story is strong enough, a project can survive for decades before making it to the big screen.

This isn't true of every story or storyteller, however. Sometimes, if a film is in development (or production) for too long, the creative spark that ignited the whole process can begin to die. That's one reason procrastination and deadlines play such critical roles in the writing life. Procrastination is the sworn enemy of motivation and will surely sap it over time if you don't remain committed to your story and get it on paper while your creative fires are still hot. Deadlines help you to get your story on paper, calling for a specific number of pages at specified times. Deadlines naturally restrain procrastination (if you let them) and enable your passion to motivate your work throughout the life of a project.

> The inclination of my life—the motto, you might call it—has been to do things and make things which will give pleasure to people in new and amusing ways. By doing that I please and satisfy myself. I think all artists—whether they paint, write, sing or play music, write for the theater or movies, make poetry or sculpture—all of these are first of all pleasure-givers. People who like to bring delight to other people, and hereby gain pleasure and satisfaction for themselves.
>
> —Walt Disney

There can come a point where even the most passionate of storytellers feel they have given all they have to a particular project, and begin to lose that passion, whether they are consciously aware of it or not. One sure sign that you may have overstayed your welcome is when the writing process ceases to be fun and starts to really feel like work. Make no mistake, writing *is* hard work and always will be. It just shouldn't *feel* like it, at least not very often. If you get to a point where you can't make a distinction between writing a movie and punching a time clock, it might be best to turn your attention to something that will reignite the creative spark within you.

Storytellers must learn to recognize when it's time to move on to a new project. Sometimes it's because the story or characters just don't seem as interesting or compelling as they once did, and it's time to bring in some fresh eyes to take a more objective look at them. At other times, it's because the movie you're making no longer bears much resemblance to the one that inspired you in the first place. The end result is the same in either case: pass the torch or snuff it out. You're not doing yourself or the project any good by stubbornly clinging to something that's not working or, at least, not working for *you*.

After co-directing *The Lion King*, Roger Allers wanted to tell an epic tale of mistaken identity set against the backdrop of the ancient Inca civilization in South America. The main plot concerned a haughty emperor (voiced by David Spade) who trades places with a peasant (originally voiced by Owen Wilson), learning about life, love, and leadership in the process. At its core, it was a story about a common man teaching an arrogant man how to be a good leader. There was also a love story subplot and the Jafar-like machinations of a witch named Yzma (Eartha Kitt).

The first story-reel screening for the studio brass did not go well at all (much like early screenings of *The Great Mouse Detective*, *Aladdin*, and any number of other eventual hits). Roger was philosophical about the studio's poor response to *Kingdom of the Sun*, knowing that, as painful as it can be, the process does reveal what is working in a film as well as what needs to be changed or cut altogether. After the studio had extensively reworked the story, the only element remaining from the original version was the notion of the prince getting turned into a llama by the conniving, power-hungry witch in an effort to steal the throne. For Allers, the story no longer moved him. It was at this point that he decided he did not want to commit years of his career to a project he was no longer passionate about. It wasn't the epic tale of mistaken identity that Allers originally envisioned, but a light comedy that was more of a showcase for the comedic vocal stylings of David Spade. Allers walked away from the film, leaving his co-director, Mark Dindal, to complete the film that would become *The Emperor's New Groove*.

You have to be passionate about the stories you want to tell and desperate to get them onscreen, from the first word on that blank page to the rolling of the end credits. Your passion is your motivation. It's the one friend you can count on to get you through the various legs of your own hero's journey, from those initial 120 pages through the false hopes and false starts of development hell to the alternating agony and ecstasy of production itself.

## The End of the Beginning ......................

> *Somehow I can't believe there are many heights that can't be scaled by a man who knows the secret of making dreams come true. This special secret, it seems to me, can be summarized in four C's. They are Curiosity, Confidence, Courage, and Constancy, and the greatest of these is Confidence. When you believe a thing, believe it all over, implicitly and unquestioningly.*
>
> —Walt Disney

In this chapter, we've examined the culmination of your creative journey. Writing a screenplay can be a long, winding, and lonely road, and confidence clearly leads the way en route. Writers must have the confidence to sit down and tell a story. Even more to the point, they must have the confidence that they can and will do whatever it takes to tell that story the best possible way. And that takes courage.

The key to any kind of success in show business is persistence, or, in the parlance of Walt's four C's, constancy. It's important when you're an aspiring writer, and even more important when you're a working writer. Whether you write for an hour a day, or one weekend a month; whether you write plot first, or develop the characters, or explore a theme, you must find the time and the discipline to "start doing," in Walt's words. Constancy also applies directly to the story you're telling—each character must be constant in their personality and actions, and the story must be constantly moving forward, building upon itself, until it reaches its inevitable conclusion.

To these four C's, I'd like to suggest a fifth: change. Change is an inevitable part of the creative process and the writer must be ready for it. "The leap from word to imagery is a process of discovery," says producer Don Hahn. "It's like leaving for a long vacation to Europe. You start out with your tickets, and your traveler's checks and itinerary, and clean laundry, and you come home and you've lost your luggage and you've spent all your money, but you have really great pictures to recall the trip. The travel is the most enjoyable when you can roll with the punches and accept the fact that along the way you're going to have changes. You're going to go to a town, but it's going to be raining. Or you go to a museum, and find it's closed. Perhaps you'll make reservations at a restaurant that everybody said was good and it won't be so good. But another time you'll stop in a café that looks like a hole in the wall and you'll have the best

> *I can never stand still. I must explore and experiment. I am never satisfied with my work. I resent the limitations of my own imagination.*
>
> —Walt Disney

experience of your whole vacation. That's exactly what making a movie is like. That sort of chaotic thing may drive people nuts, but it's important. You have to be willing and understand that you're probably going to end up exploring all those cafés. You're going to have some laid-out plans, battle plans, you might say, but there's an amount of chaos that goes along with it and that's really a positive thing."[115]

Walt's fourth C is curiosity, and it certainly played an important role in his own life and career. It was the "fuel" of his imagination. That is because curiosity has more to do with personality and lifestyle than art or craft. It concerns your own personal philosophies about life and people, and the way you look at the world. Curiosity is what makes art possible, so it's a trait that any artist needs to cultivate and nourish in order to interpret the world around them, ask their probing questions, and explore universal truths.

Screenwriters in particular seem to have a natural curiosity about who people are, how things work, and why things are the way they are. They ask themselves those questions and then attempt to answer them through their work on behalf of the world. Writers in any medium must spend as much time observing the world around them as they do looking within, as any artist must do in the creation of their work. In that way, curiosity is every bit as important as the raw creative talent that enables writers to do what they do, and the two are so intricately intertwined that it's impossible to separate them.

"I'm just very curious," Walt said. "Got to find out what makes things tick. I've always liked working with my hands; my father was a carpenter. I even apprenticed to my own machine shop here and learned the trade. Since my outlook and attitudes are ingrained throughout our organization, all our people have this curiosity; it keeps us moving forward, exploring, experimenting, opening new doors."

Curiosity is indeed what "keeps us moving forward, exploring, experimenting, opening new doors." Walt Disney was a living example of one of his most important philosophies. His whole career revolved around what came next, the new worlds that remained to conquer once the previous one had been vanquished. He started with short cartoons, giving them story and character and sound and color. Then he set about making them compelling enough to tell feature-length stories, using three-dimensional characters, music, and technology to make each one better than the last.

When Walt had done everything he felt he could do in animated and live-action films, he moved into two different mediums entirely: television and theme parks. No longer were his stories confined to a movie screen. Now he could bring stories directly into people's homes and place the audience in the three-dimensional environment of his stories. At the time of his death, he was deep into figuring out how he could take everything he had learned in entertainment and make life itself better for his audience, a more accurate reflection of the idealized worlds seen in his entertainment, perhaps. Everything Walt did was fueled by his insatiable curiosity, propelling himself ever higher in terms of his goals, and ever deeper within himself to find the creative spirit to accomplish them.

"All creative people must find that same spirit of exploration and discovery within them," said Walt, "and unleash the curiosity it inspires. It's in there, or you wouldn't feel compelled to share your stories with the world in the first place. Your own curiosity will provide the raw materials you need to do that. Ideas are all around you. Your stories already exist and they're everywhere, living in the people you meet and the things you do. It's up to you to find them, interpret them, and share them. And an insatiable curiosity will lead you right to them."

While first on Walt's list, curiosity is the perfect place to end our exploration of Disney storytelling because it is also where it begins. It is the creative impulse that leads people to a life in storytelling, and it will be a constant presence on your own Hero's Journey. The big question now is what will your journey be like? What will you discover? What will move you enough to share it with the world? What form will it take?

The answer, such as it is, is a reassuring one. Your journey can be whatever you want it to be, and your work should reflect that. Everyone's journey is completely different and the variety of our paths is what has enabled us to create thousands of years' worth of art, and untold millions of stories. That means that there are untold millions more waiting to be discovered, and you will have the opportunity to tell a few of them in a way that will be unique to you. Never cease to be curious. Have confidence that what interests you will also speak to millions of others. Be constant in the execution of your ideas, whatever form they may take. And always live and work courageously.

# Fade Out: An Author's Journey ·················

**W**riting this book was a journey of discovery not dissimilar to the one undertaken by screenwriters when they set out to write a script. I had a vague notion of the story I wanted to tell and the characters that would help me do that. But, for the most part, it was like watching a new film for the first time, one that revealed itself to me beat by beat, scene by scene, act by act.

The story began to take me by surprise, as any good tale will, assuming a life of its own and telling *me* what it wanted and needed to be rather than the other way around. It came to life. I began to serve the story and stopped trying to impose my will upon it. The ever evolving central question was, "Just what kind of story is it that we're telling here?" It turned out that there were a number of different answers to that question, and each one of them was correct in its own way.

There were times when I felt the book suffered from something of a multiple personality disorder. Was it a screenwriting textbook? I hoped not, because I had little interest in writing one of those, and we all know the world doesn't need another one. Was it more of a history book about process, story, and script according to Disney? I had much more interest in something like that, because show business history has shown that Disney has obviously been doing something right for the past seventy-five years. Or was it more of an inspirational think piece, a "This is how Disney does it and maybe, just maybe, you can do it, too" collection of encouraging words? The answer changed constantly throughout the writing of the book.

Ultimately I think it is a magical alchemy (you just knew *that* was going to come up again) of all those things, making it unique among books of its kind. There is a little something in here for a number of different audiences. The book's historical perspective is obviously going to be of interest to fans and students of Disney. It is the first work about Disney to concentrate exclusively on storytelling and to view the animated features from story and script standpoints as opposed to focusing on the visual elements—the "art making"—or the artists themselves.

Beyond the more obvious historical elements, there is also plenty of educational and inspirational material for both aspiring and professional writers. This is where an examination of the overall Disney process came into play. The unique approach to story and character that the studio has taken throughout its history sets examples that will serve *any* writer well, in animation or live-action, film or television, on the stage or in the pages of a novel. Although each of those mediums possesses its own strengths and weaknesses and appeals to different writers for different reasons, ultimately storytelling is storytelling, and the Disney process offers a number of compelling truths that can be applied equally well to all of them.

However you came to this story and for whatever reason, I hope you found what you were looking for in these pages. So many different artists—and the characters and stories they share with us—play such important roles at just the right moments in our lives. I know the storytellers at Disney—from every decade—have played a significant role in my life as a writer; the fact that you've chosen to hear their story tells me the same is true for you. I hope that in some small way this book helps illuminate how they've made such an impact on so many over the years.

Now, put down the book and go pick up a pen or turn on the computer. There are a lot of people out there just waiting to enjoy a good story. . . .

# Disney Animated Features...

| | |
|---|---|
| *Snow White and the Seven Dwarfs* | 1937 |
| *Pinocchio* | 1940 |
| *Fantasia* | 1940 |
| *Dumbo* | 1941 |
| *Bambi* | 1942 |
| *Saludos Amigos* | 1943 |
| *The Three Caballeros* | 1945 |
| *Make Mine Music* | 1946 |
| *Fun and Fancy Free* | 1947 |
| *Melody Time* | 1948 |
| *The Adventures of Ichabod and Mr. Toad* | 1949 |
| *Cinderella* | 1950 |
| *Alice In Wonderland* | 1951 |
| *Peter Pan* | 1953 |
| *Lady and the Tramp* | 1955 |
| *Sleeping Beauty* | 1959 |
| *101 Dalmatians* | 1961 |
| *The Sword in the Stone* | 1963 |
| *The Jungle Book* | 1967 |
| *The Aristocats* | 1970 |
| *Robin Hood* | 1973 |
| *The Many Adventures of Winnie the Pooh* | 1977 |

| | |
|---|---|
| *The Rescuers* | 1977 |
| *The Fox and the Hound* | 1981 |
| *The Black Cauldron* | 1985 |
| *The Great Mouse Detective* | 1986 |
| *Oliver & Company* | 1988 |
| *The Little Mermaid* | 1989 |
| *The Rescuers Down Under* | 1990 |
| *Beauty and the Beast* | 1991 |
| *Aladdin* | 1992 |
| *The Lion King* | 1994 |
| *Pocahontas* | 1995 |
| *The Hunchback of Notre Dame* | 1996 |
| *Hercules* | 1997 |
| *Mulan* | 1998 |
| *Tarzan* | 1999 |
| *Fantasia/2000* | 2000 |
| *The Emperor's New Groove* | 2000 |
| *Atlantis: The Lost Empire* | 2001 |
| *Lilo & Stitch* | 2002 |
| *Treasure Planet* | 2002 |
| *Brother Bear* | 2003 |
| *Home on the Range* | 2004 |

# Endnotes .....................................

## THE WORD ACCORDING TO WALT

1   *It All Started with a Mouse: The Disney Story,* produced and directed by
    Alan Benson, packaged for The Disney Channel by G-Man Productions
    (copyright © The Walt Disney Company 1989).
2   Ibid.

## INSPIRATION

3   Unpublished interview for *Treasure Planet: A Voyage of Discovery,*
    by Jeff Kurtti (Disney Editions, 2002).
4   *Hercules: The Chaos of Creation,* by Stephen Rebello and
    Jane Healey (Hyperion, 1997).
5   Unpublished interview for *Treasure Planet: A Voyage of Discovery,*
    by Jeff Kurtti (Disney Editions, 2002).
6   *The Art of Mulan,* by Jeff Kurtti (Hyperion, 1998).
7   *Disney's Art of Animation: From Mickey Mouse to Beauty and the Beast,*
    by Bob Thomas (Hyperion, 1991).
8   Ibid.
9   Ibid.
10  *The Art of Mulan,* by Jeff Kurtti (Hyperion, 1998).
11  Author interview with Chris Sanders.
12  *Lilo & Stitch: Collected Stories from the Film's Creators,*
    edited by Clark Wakabayashi (Disney Editions, 2002).
13  Ibid.
14  Ibid.
15  Ibid.
16  Author interview with Mary-Jane Ruggels.

## PERSPIRATION

17  Author interview with Don Hahn.
18  Author interview with Roy E. Disney.
19  Author interview with Joe Grant.
20  *It All Started with a Mouse: The Disney Story,* produced and directed
    by Alan Benson, packaged for The Disney Channel by G-Man Productions
    (copyright © The Walt Disney Company 1989).
21  *Walt Disney's Nine Old Men,* by John Canemaker (Disney Editions,
    October 2001).
22  *Disney's Art of Animation: From Mickey Mouse to Beauty and the Beast,*
    by Bob Thomas (Hyperion, 1991).

23  *It All Started with a Mouse: The Disney Story,* produced and directed by Alan Benson, packaged for The Disney Channel by G-Man Productions (copyright © The Walt Disney Company 1989).

24  *Disney's Art of Animation: From Mickey Mouse to Beauty and the Beast,* by Bob Thomas (Hyperion, 1991).

25  Ibid.

26  *The Tarzan Chronicles,* by Howard E. Green (Hyperion, 1999).

27  *Hercules: The Chaos of Creation,* by Stephen Rebello and Jane Healey (Hyperion, 1997).

28  Author interview with Chuck Williams.

29  *The Art of Pocahontas,* by Stephen Rebello (Hyperion, 1995).

30  Ibid.

31  Author interview with Roy E. Disney.

32  *The Tarzan Chronicles,* by Howard E. Green (Hyperion, 1999).

33  Ibid.

34  Author interview with Chris Sanders.

35  *Disney's Art of Animation: From Mickey Mouse to Hercules,* by Bob Thomas (Hyperion, 1992, 1997).

36  *The Art of The Lion King,* by Christopher Finch (Hyperion, 1994).

37  Author interview with Don Hahn.

38  *The Lion King* Special Edition DVD, distributed by Buena Vista Home Entertainment, Inc. (copyright © Disney 2003).

39  *The Art of Pocahontas,* by Stephen Rebello (Hyperion, 1995).

40  *The Art of The Lion King,* by Christopher Finch (Hyperion, 1994).

41  *The Art of Pocahontas,* by Stephen Rebello (Hyperion, 1995).

42  Unpublished interview for *Treasure Planet: A Voyage of Discovery,* by Jeff Kurtti (Disney Editions, 2002).

43  *Storytelling in Animation: The Art of the Animated Image, vol. 2: An Anthology,* edited by John Canemaker (American Film Institute, 1988).

44  Author interview with Glen Keane.

45  *Aladdin: The Making of an Animated Film,* by John Culhane (Hyperion, 1992).

46  *The Art of The Little Mermaid,* by Jeff Kurtti (Hyperion, 1997).

47  Author interview with Chris Sanders.

48  *The Disney Villains,* by Frank Thomas and Ollie Johnston (Hyperion, 1993).

49  *The Disney Films, Fourth Edition,* by Leonard Maltin (Disney Editions, 2000).

50  *The Disney Villains,* by Frank Thomas and Ollie Johnston (Hyperion, 1993).

51    Ibid.
52    Author interview with Don Hahn.
53    *The Disney Villains,* by Frank Thomas and Ollie Johnston (Hyperion, 1993).
54    Ibid.
55    *Walt Disney: The Art of Animation,* by Bob Thomas (Golden Press, 1958).
56    Author interview with Broose Johnson.
57    Author interview with Chris Sanders.
58    *The Art of The Hunchback of Notre Dame,* by Stephen Rebello (Hyperion, 1996).
59    Author interview with Broose Johnson.
60    *Storytelling in Animation: The Art of the Animated Image, vol. 2: An Anthology,* edited by John Canemaker (American Film Institute, 1988).
61    *Hercules: The Chaos of Creation,* by Stephen Rebello and Jane Healey (Hyperion, 1997).
62    *The Tarzan Chronicles,* by Howard E. Green (Hyperion, 1999).
63    Ibid.
64    *Aladdin: The Making of an Animated Film,* by John Culhane (Hyperion, 1992).
65    Ibid.
66    Author interview with Chuck Williams.
67    Author interview with Don Hahn.
68    Ibid.
69    *The Lion King* Special Edition DVD, distributed by Buena Vista Home Entertainment, Inc. (copyright © Disney 2003).
70    *Disney's Art of Animation: From Mickey Mouse to Hercules,* by Bob Thomas (Hyperion, 1992, 1997).
71    *The Lion King* Special Edition DVD, distributed by Buena Vista Home Entertainment, Inc. (copyright © Disney 2003).
72    Author interview with Don Hahn.
73    *Disney's Art of Animation: From Mickey Mouse to Hercules,* by Bob Thomas (Hyperion, 1992, 1997).
74    Author interview with Don Hahn.
75    *The Art of the Lion King,* by Christopher Finch (Hyperion, 1994).
76    *The Lion King* Special Edition DVD, distributed by Buena Vista Home Entertainment, Inc. (copyright © Disney 2003).
77    Ibid.
78    Ibid.
79    Ibid.
80    Ibid.
81    Ibid.
82    Ibid.
83    Ibid.
84    *Disney's Animation Magic,* by Don Hahn (Hyperion, 1996, 2000).
85    *The Tarzan Chronicles,* by Howard E. Green (Hyperion, 1999).

86  *Aladdin: The Making of an Animated Film*, by John Culhane (Hyperion, 1992).

87  Author interview with Chris Sanders.

88  *The Lion King* Special Edition DVD, distributed by Buena Vista Home Entertainment, Inc. (copyright © Disney 2003).

89  Author interview with Ron Clements.

90  *The Art of The Lion King*, by Christopher Finch (Hyperion, 1994).

91  *The Tarzan Chronicles*, by Howard E. Green (Hyperion, 1999).

92  *Brother Bear: A Transformation Tale*, by Clark Wakabayashi (Disney Editions, 2003).

93  *The Art of The Lion King*, by Christopher Finch (Hyperion, 1994).

94  *Brother Bear: A Transformation Tale*, by Clark Wakabayashi (Disney Editions, 2003).

## CULMINATION

95  *The Lion King* Special Edition DVD, distributed by Buena Vista Home Entertainment, Inc. (copyright © Disney 2003).

96  *Aladdin: The Making of an Animated Film*, by John Culhane (Hyperion, 1992).

97  Author interview with John Musker.

98  *Aladdin: The Making of an Animated Film*, by John Culhane (Hyperion, 1992).

99  Author interview with John Musker.

100  *Disney's Art of Animation: From Mickey Mouse to Hercules*, by Bob Thomas (Hyperion, 1992, 1997).

101  Unpublished interview for *Treasure Planet: A Voyage of Discovery*, by Jeff Kurtti (Disney Editions, 2002).

102  *Aladdin: The Making of an Animated Film*, by John Culhane (Hyperion, 1992).

103  Author interview with Chris Sanders.

104  Ibid.

105  Ibid.

106  Ibid.

107  Ibid.

108  Ibid.

109  *Brother Bear: A Transformation Tale*, by Clark Wakabayashi (Disney Editions, 2003).

110  Author interview with Chuck Williams.

111  Author interview with Ron Clements.

112  Ibid.

113  Author interview with Roy E. Disney.

114  Ibid.

115  Author interview with Don Hahn.

# Index ········································

Photo Credit: Michael Roddy

Jason Surrell is a show writer at Walt Disney Imagineering, the creative force behind Walt Disney Parks and Resorts. He is the author of *The Haunted Mansion: From The Magic Kingdom to the Movies*, *The Art of The Haunted Mansion*, and was a contributing essayist to *The Imagineering Way*.

He has written for Walt Disney Television's internationally syndicated series *Secrets of the Animal Kingdom*, and wrote, directed, and co-produced a comedy that premiered at the 2001 New York International Independent Film and Video Festival. Jason currently has a number of animated and live-action film projects in various stages of development. He is also working on two books about the Pirates of the Caribbean attraction and films.

Jason lives in Orlando, Florida, with his wife, Christy, and their dog, Padmé.